Black

Dresses

Stain

by

Chalet Jean-Baptiste

Written In the Spirit LLC
@2018, 2ND EDITION
© 2006 Chalet Tranumn
All Rights Reserved.

ISBN: 978-1-7327031-1-7
Library of Congress Control Number: 2006925485

Printed in the United States of America

*This book is dedicated to my daughter, Ariana.
You are so beautiful. In your eyes,
I see myself- strong and fearless. Never settle
for less. You are a Queen-in–the-making.*

Body...or Mind

"Of course, I swallow," she said. "Anything to please."

And they never seemed to see past these words. She listened to Mozart, Beethoven, all the classical favorites. She studied their lives and could even play some of their tunes. Her mother bought her a black baby grand piano. She had the ability to pick up the notes as if they had quietly danced in front of her. She would peacefully listen to America's favorite composers and skillfully point out their intricacies. Her teacher called her a musical genius with a trained ear. She could even sing when she wanted to—a tone beautiful enough to be recognized among a choir of voices.

Instead she told them, "I can make you scream and moan like a baby. I can teach you how to sing in bed."

Shakespeare, Hawthorne, Thoreau, Emerson, Woolf, Rich, Poe—she had read them all. She understood them and could recite their prose as though she had written it herself. She even started a book club for the neighborhood intellects. She dictated quotes from authors who had made a difference in her life—Angelou, Shange, Morrison, Tan, Walker, and Vanzant. In her down time, she would meditate on the essence of their words. She would concentrate on the meaning of their unfamiliar vocabulary. But she never reflected long enough to discover the truth about herself. She never looked hard enough to remember the pain in her eyes. So whenever she opened her mouth, instead of screaming as she had wanted to, instead of letting the world hear her tumultuous voice when reciting beautiful poetry, she found herself kissing and sucking and saying all the wrong things.

When she was a child, her parents never missed a dance recital, and she never missed a class. As she grew older, she became more graceful in every step and more passionate with every choreography. Many times the moves just came to her. The rhythm was innate. And when she danced, the room starting spinning, voices grew quiet, and attention belonged to her. But she wanted only the attention of them.

"I can swing around a pole and dance for you. I can do you real good."

She was a natural. She believed in no makeup, no perm, righteous causes, peace, open sexuality, and freedom. She was the center of a social or political debate. When she raised her voice, everyone listened because she always had a lot to say. She was professor and counselor to many—always offering words of wisdom. She had enough insight to tell you the solutions to your problems. Many said that she could see what was not always visible. That someone had whispered the truth in her ear to reveal the unknown.

She rarely missed a Sunday church service and was Sunday's best dressed. She wore colorful yet subtle suits with wide-brimmed hats. She always joined the prayer line—offering one and receiving another. When the pastor said something that struck a cord, she would yell "Amen." She never talked too much to the church folks because even though the pastor saw something very spiritual in her, she said that the members didn't have their leader's heart. That they wore masks, different than hers.

When asked who she was, she said, " So many things. So many things I could be to you."

Different degrees, moods, and styles had made her eccentric without being shallow. It never seemed to affect her that her life lacked permanency. Change was normal and the only thing that wasn't… was monogamy.

"Of course, I'm a freak," she answered whenever they asked. It was all they ever asked because they believed it was all she could offer.

The City Never Sleeps

Sandra never could get away from the city streets. No matter how many times she'd run away, she learned that the city had become a part of her being. Her mind took on its own personalities wherever she would go. It became nauseating with memory in New York City, dreamfully awakening in Newark, and painfully reassuring in Philadelphia. Nothing could satisfy the soul as the city could. Despite the many places where she slept, nothing could make her experience ecstasy and torture the way she did in New York. It was in New York that everything came back to her mind—all the memories. It was here that her pen could tell the stories.

She got on the Greyhound bus from Philadelphia to New York and thought about the change she would undergo coming from two different environments. Just as her thoughts began to make any sense, a sophisticated looking, tall man sat next to her.

"Hello. Seat taken?" he asked.

Though she had hoped for a seat to herself, she hated when people acted as though they were entitled to two seats. "No," she answered, "be my guest."

"Richard," he said extending his hand.

Not wanting to know why he introduced himself, she reluctantly replied, "Sandra."

Much to her surprise, what first began as a boring introduction turned into an engaging, intriguing conversation. He told her about his college life, his family, his belief in Christ, and his philosophy on relationships and marriage. She, in return, shared her views. His thinking was unlike that of an ordinary man. He possessed passion and femininity. He loved the African-American women while realizing their flaws. He was as respectful as a 1960s family man with the sudden twist and openness of the millennium man. He was fine, and the best thing about that was that he seemed to not notice it. He admitted his insecurities yet showed only the secure. He listened and looked directly into her pupils as if she didn't have to say a word because he already understood. When he wasn't looking, she found herself smiling. His humor made her laugh...laugh freely.

"Richard," she thought, "was a subject for her writing."

Just as she began to doze off, she was awakened by the noise as the bus pulled in to the Port Authority Terminal. She was going to see him. He was all she ever thought about. Her parents lived not too far away and she dared not make them aware that their only child was coming home without seeing them, especially to go and visit him. So she often tip-toed her way around the city hoping not to run into any family or friends of the family. Tony often picked her up from the bus station. Whenever their eyes met, they smiled. The days apart seemed to only make the weekends more intense.

"Baby, how was the ride?" he asked, as he intently eyed her and everyone in her vicinity.

"Great. Just happy to see you. Missed you much. I felt my body call for you a couple of times this week."

He kissed her. "Missed you, too."

Richard, coming off the bus, caught her eye to give her his final look. Tony must have caught the glitter in her eye because his smile left his face. He looked around and with each moment of searching, Sandra could see Tony's demeanor begin to change.

"Who was that that caught your attention?" he impatiently asked.

"Oh, just someone I met on the bus. Nice guy," she answered.

"So how exactly did ya'll meet? And what makes him so nice?"

This was the part that made her not want to stay. So often, he would get like this and when he did, she'd envision herself turning into a bird and flying over the city. "He sat next to me on the bus and we talked."

Tony's face immediately turned into what looked like the beginning of drama. He searched for Richard as if he wanted to question his intentions. When he realized he was gone, Tony, unsatisfied, stated, "Ohh, so, you make it a habit to talk to strangers."

She, wishing to avoid the drama, replied, "No."

During the whole train ride to his house, they were silent. She made sure to keep her head in a book or in Tony's face so that there would be no unwanted conversation or incidents. Then, finally, she said, "Maybe we can go to catch a movie tonight."

"Okay, sounds like a plan," he said, giving her a half a smile.

Walking up to his house, she hoped that his mother wasn't home. Sandra had so desperately wanted to spend a quiet evening together. His mother, a Jehovah's Witness, was a major roadblock in her 20-year-old son's personal and sex life. Tony would often have to sneak his affections for Sandra and it annoyed the hell out of her. Of course, she was happy when she realized that it was just the two of them. She entered his tiny bedroom where she had spent many summer days.

Her mind slipped to those summer days when she would kill and die for him. He was street and she was class. She was Rhythm & Blues and he was Rap. She introduced him to suits and he told her it was okay to wear sneakers. She thought that a good Christian girl shouldn't give head and he showed her that there was no relationship without it. Tony made her feel as if her regretfully, recently cut short hair made her look beautiful. He brought out the ghetto in her and said it made her look like a queen. She told him all her secrets—all the ones she couldn't tell anyone else (that the streets were already a part of her, that they had without notice sculpted her, and that she had become a master of covering it up). Somewhere in between she became weaker and he stronger. She learned how to scream and cry when it really hurt. He taught her how to curse with meaning and introduced her to drama. She was renamed concubine and he crowned king. She told him about the sexual abuse and promiscuity. She let him in on the family relationship that was anything but perfect. After three years of him off and on again puppet-mastering her, she had now become his zombie, unable to let go. She loved and hated, adored and despised him.

This spring day she immediately began to make love with him because that's what they always did first if his mother wasn't home. She was passionately engaged, closing her eyes. Her tears welled up but she held them back. She couldn't explain them. All she knew was how much she loved Tony and how she felt she needed him. He intoxicated her. "Damn, how good this feels," she moaned as she released her body, mind, and soul to him. He made her forget about the city.

Afterward, he held her, pulled her closer to him, and whispered in her ear, "So, did you give him your number?"

"Give who my number?" she asked.

"The nice guy on the bus. Was he nice enough to get your number?"

"It wasn't like that. It was just a conversation. I didn't get to know him or anything."

"What kind of conversation?" he probed.

She tried to pull away but he held tighter. "About the things in life like beliefs and stuff like that. Nothing important."

"Things like sex. And how you love it when a man goes downtown? Did you tell him that you can ride a man all night?"

"No," she quietly answered.

She could feel his anger intensify. She wondered where it had originated and why it always appeared just when she was letting go. Within a moment's notice, he could make her forget that she was still horny and ready for round two. His hands became dirty and his touch unwanted. The tears that began to well up again took on another meaning. Her thoughts wandered to how tough the city could be. In his room, she began to feel claustrophobic. He kissed her breast. Then he proceeded to eat her out, but her orgasm felt more like a scream. When he gave his face a breath of air, she saw a demon. He pounded himself inside of her and she could no longer moan. She laid in silence until he felt complete.

"Did you tell him that you belong to me?" he asked.

On their way to the movies, she wanted to look at the people's faces. She wanted to see what freedom felt like. She wanted to experience pain, fear, and lust again. She wanted to see a man or woman's eyes to see what kept them going.

"Today will be different," she said to herself. "I will pretend that I can see their faces and that they are smiling…"

"Let's go see that new love story. Something to make us realize how good and real our love is," Tony interrupted her thoughts.

Sandra stopped and turned toward him, looked him directly in his eyes, and softly and passionately kissed him.

She turned away looking at the red light ahead of her and thought, "He's right. Richard and I do have something that is real. Our love is good."

It wasn't the first time she lied to herself but she knew the city had so much to offer. Every streetlight told a story. Every train station offered a refuge and escape. The city meant so much to her. Unfortunately, being with him meant that there were going to be some things that she was going to miss. Some stories she was not going to be able to write. And she, for the moment, was fine with that.

High Street

Utica Avenue
Waiting on the A train
Or for a rat to run by
Paper bag to blow
Trying to waste time

"Pamphlet, miss."
I stare, annoyed at interruption
She with disrupted old-lady curls
Anne Taylor, Salvation Army suit
"I already know Jesus loves me"

Brenda spends a lot of money on her hats
To hide her moving lips
Jeremy can make the keys on the piano move on their
own
But the music is so loud I can't understand the words
And Tony looks at himself too much

I have a testimony, too
Bentley, Benz, houses, land, cars, the riches of the
world
Momma Risa pulls out her pocketbook trying to find
five one-dollar bills
That try to hide from her
Ebony catches on fire every time she thinks of her
night before
Anniversary, Celebration, Special Occasion again
I'm sure Brian already smells that chicken
Cause I don't see him anymore

Did you see
Did you hear
Did you know
That I know everything because I am closer to the vine
Because my grape juice was a little stronger
Ain't he and she tellin' the truth
The Head can tell me my future and let me know about
my present
And no, I don't have a past

Open the doors
All aboard
Experience the experience

And I see the bum lying on the dark gray bench
And he smells
But I sit next to him anyway
The bag lady is talking to herself about all the "bull-
shit" in the world
The lady with the business suit doesn't want me to
touch her
And the young woman looks like her jeans are going to
bust open
The next stop is High Street
And I hold on to the pole
That I know a hundred people were touching
Because it's the only thing that will keep me standing
up

Dangerous Waters

I stood and sat and silently cried under the running waters of the close quarters of the quiet apartment. It always seemed strangely loud…but seemingly only to my ears. I heard stories from the walls. Stories full of dark tales, screams, and dramatic scenes. The sheets only changed patterns and moments but all rendered the same story. They had taught me the intensity of my longing and the strength of my desire. The neat white tiles had replaced the molded wood that marked and replayed footprints of all different sizes of what mainly consisted of working boots and delicate stilettos. Sometimes I heard the shoes, but only when I had become very silent.

Nothing could capture my thoughts or reclaim my path like the waters. The waters had shown me both fear and compassion. The many waters that I had inhabited became the essence of my stories. There in the waters I would release myself and allow my spirit to come back to my being. I became human again…a true woman…unmasked. Sometimes it scared me that the waters knew so much or that they had shared so many intimate moments with me. It was the way the sprinkles, whether delicate or hard, pricked my body while at the same time causing me to re-associate with painful experiences by temporarily stealing my mind or cleansing me of impurities.

At a tender age, the waters were present. The blood from the unwanted anal sex led me there. Later, the abortions brought me back. From time to time, when I wanted to say "no" but couldn't or wouldn't, the water would seem to wash away the fingerprints and float away the semen. When I thought I had fallen in love or after a night of incredible sex or a feeling of contentment within myself, the waters gently agreed. Then I would sing to the waters or myself in gratification.

During the summer, I would go down to the pier in Brooklyn Heights or Canarsie and listen as the waters would speak to me. Some days they would say beautiful things like "Life is wonderful" or "Men are God's gift." Other days they would say, "Jump." I never jumped because of my fear of suffocation. I didn't want to be found wrinkled, pale, floating on top of the water as though I had finally surrendered myself to Mother Nature. The funny thing is that the waters would say the same thing at the pier as in the shower at my house, depending on the communication I had shared with waters. But I'd rather hear sprinkles hit the side of my tub than hear the noise of my bedroom walls.

The bathroom tubs comprised of showers and streams made my tears invisible and moments nonexistent. They contained my ecstasy and allowed me to express my happiness. They always floated away, always ceased to flow. And this it how it was…of my joy…and my pain.

It's a wonder that the intimacy I shared with the waters was not always consistent. I never learned how to swim. Even when I was sent away to camp and my swimming instructor threw me in the water, I never could grasp the concept of floating. The water frightened me in that it had the innate ability to take life away…that one's spirit could lose a fight.

I thought about how easy it was for someone or

something to steal my spirit. Whenever it would come, it came like a ghost, without warning and with full force. I felt it coming as I always do. When I should have been silent, I screamed and shouted. But there were those times when I silently buried my spirit. Like the time I had just given birth to my first child and realized he wasn't there. Or the nights he never came home, or the first blow to my head by a man I lived for or when I found out he was having a baby and then another baby.

I can't explain what comes over me, but I know I've had private ceremonies for my spirit plenty of times. I kept on pushing because no matter what state my spirit was in, my body had never failed me. As long as my body was presentable, I could act as if the spirit was still there. I said that I would never fight over the love of a man. I said that I would never let anyone get the best of me. I said that I valued myself the best, but I lay on this cold wooden floor all out of words. I, who once thought I was barren, was finished with abortion #3.

I was laughing hysterically that brilliant me keeps playing a fool. The pattern has continued, and I am speechless. No more grandiose wisdom to give now. My girlfriend, Felicia was getting tired of my shit. She wanted to know why I had let "these niggahs take up so much space in my life." I told her, "They stole my eyes and my spirit can't seem to find them." But I lied.

I always saw it coming before it did, and my spirit warned me. But I fell for the moments, and the moments loved me back. I should have earned an Oscar the way I painted on my smiles, the way I made them think that they never really mattered to me—that I didn't let them affect my esteem. I told them that my spirit had special ingredients: "Brick walls."

Sometimes when I was experiencing a moment of joy, my spirit would dance. It was those walks in the park, deep conversations, new love, a call from an old friend, a church service, a comedic moment between Felicia and I, two-hour talks with my mom reminding me of better days, a song on the answering machine from my father reminding me of Farmers Blvd. and Bible games, a day when my grandmother said I looked good, and my daughter's eyes. When I looked at her I was transferring the only spirit that was still left—the part that danced. But I know there were moments that she walked in on my funeral services.

Today, I don't remember how I made it home or how I walked down Malcolm X Blvd. in so much pain. I could feel my mind paralyzed from staring at the wooden floor. It had been almost an hour before I realized that the water had been running. I stood up and wanted to run away, but I couldn't. I took off my clothes and stared at my run-down, overworked body that had been life-stretched. I stepped into the steamy bathtub and drew on the white tiles the words, "What now?" I watched the clots fall out of me.

In the silence of the waters, I prayed that they would wash it all away.

Unconditional Love

Nevertheless, his tenderness embraces me with arms of
cold passion
I know this love is eccentric, full of canards from the
past
Stories yet to be told
Yet to acknowledge the stubborn hidden things
Love always seems to hide
The passion deep within is filled with doubt that this
feeling may go away
Please stay!
No more temporary highs
Let my lows be filled with love for you
I can hear your tears as they cry for me
Can you feel mine?
Did you hear my heart cry for ecstasy?
Oh, the joy you bring
Yet deep inside I carry a stain of sorrow
Intimate pain to be unshared
I mask your love with laughter
And I know I yearn to hear fulfillment in your voice
More fulfillment in myself
I can't believe you're not psychic
Not capable of reading my mind
To know how my heart feels for you and my body flows
for you
And my mind wanders through the pain of naturality
for your touch
For your complete intimacy
Don't only see my face
But search my eyes for my totality

Never only see what others see but see through my
fleshly domain of vulnerability
Please caress me in your strong spirit
Never let me stray from thee
For even I understand my naivete
See my scars as victory
Never classify me
See me uniquely
Read my heart with discernment
And let not the blood that drips from it stain thee
For I shall dance in thanks for your unconditional love
For seeing beyond visibilty
Yes, I shall love you unconditionally

Other Side

Saks Fifth Avenue
Only Lord & Taylor's
Ann Taylor just won't do

Prada this
Gucci that
Your booty's phat

You toss your long bleached blonde hair
In my face and say
Paul Mitchell's a personal friend
So your hair is never thin

Ha, ha—Olive Garden is so ghetto cheap
Let's sip the oldest Chardonnay
On my porch
Or balcony
Or in the library built for the cat

"I've been out of the country, too"
But you never hear a word
'Cause your eyes are focused on my second-hand shoes

"You're so cynical"
You say
"And the reason why you do so poorly in life
Is because you are so cliché"

"Your writing is never focused or concise
And you would do so much better

If you weren't so angry"

"I can make you be…"

I'm not a lesbian
So I'm not going to pretend to be
For the Lesbian Society
Or for your boyfriend Billy Dee

You say you're on Prozac
'Cause daddy cheats on your mommy
And forgot that diamond when you were 10
And if your Ritalin doesn't kick in
You might be found skinny dipping and slapping your
mama

"This is so lame"
And the only thing fun is your high
"This is so stupid"
And the only thing smart is your lies
"This is so ugly"
And the only thing beautiful is your skin
"That is so old"
And the only thing new is your breast

You never read the paper
Because it makes you so damn depressed
You turn to me and ask, "Is it bad on the other side?"
"The other side?" I ask
"I thought this was the other side."

Bulletproof Souls

Yesterday bore memories of pain and the past lay distant, unresolved, waiting to be cast out into an unknown. She said that she would not let it get the best of her. But it would appear sporadically on her mind. She doesn't quite remember how or when it all started to fall apart. Maybe it was the rape at 13 or her first real sexual experience at 14. She had made a covenant to stay as pure as she used to be. She tried to remember being whole. But with being whole and pure came rejection. Whenever you were trying to be right, the wrong was standing there waiting to jump on your back. Virgins are laughed at but hoes are scorned. The harsh reality of a real world. They (the church people) called her different. They threw garbage cans on her, humiliated, fondled, and tormented her. Her mother said it was because she was special—that she possessed something so extraordinary it made them mad. She said that with her greatness came sorrow and being different brought persecution, but the reward would be worth it. But she didn't believe. Back in the days when mom was too strong and dad was too weak and grandma was the savior, she couldn't explain her need to continue searching. So at 14, she encountered a journey in search of her identity.

He was from church. "A Brother in Christ," he said. He would shield her and teach her the ways of the Lord as he had proclaimed. She confided in him and he poured out his love for her. Every time she ran into trouble he was there with some warm and wise words.

"Come over," he said. "Let's pray and talk and figure

things out."

She traveled from Brooklyn to Queens on the E train all the way to his house. Upon her approach, he smiled as though she was dinner. Five days he held her captive. This 36-year-old ex-policeman sent her home in bloodied panties from the anal sex he had forced on her.

"Baby, you're a woman. You can take it," he said through her screams.

She remembered the gun he used to play Russian Roulette with her head. He put her in two ponytails and gave her a shower but it never stopped the bleeding. All she kept thinking was that she hoped it would not leak on her clothes during the ride home.

After that her needs began to change. She went from the naïve, affectionate, oversensitive child who loved being loved to not understanding what love was. Not even wanting it. Love had become a failure—a hoax. Throughout her life she made many fall in love with her but she was too stoned to love back. She would just stare at them and wonder why they were so stupid to love a mere hourglass. She was incapable of kissing them or touching them with an intense passion. An orgasm confused her and she laughed if they enjoyed it too much. She became a walking secret lifestyle. Some men tried to reason with her. Some knew there was something really missing and tried unsuccessfully to make her whole.

But the only thing that satisfied her were the moments she shared with God. She could cry with him. Sometimes people would think she was talking to herself and they'd call her "crazy." She didn't care; He was all she had. Those days she felt like taking her life, she'd feel someone come up beside her and wrap their arms around her. Though none was visibly there, she know it was Him. Somedays, she screamed at Him for letting her life be so miserable but He never stopped loving…and neither did she. But God could not be touched or seen—and so she patiently waited for the moments He decided to talk to her. Sex vs. Love vs. Infatuation vs. Lust—it had all confused her. Sex was easy—real easy—too easy to explain. Love was hard. Its action came without warning to rob the self of will, choice, and reason.

By now her family was frantic. No one openly admitted the promiscuity and abuse. They took her to about five different counselors and a psychiatrist, but nothing worked. She would disappear from time to time, not only physically but also emotionally. Her mind would slip from her hands. Her family wondered where they went wrong. They had sent her to the best of schools, enrolled her in all the latest contests, sent her to ballet school and piano lessons, and never missed a Sunday service. They wanted a picture-perfect "star" child, and she disappointed them. She cussed like a sailor, dressed provocatively, fought whomever messed with her, and could support them from all the money she was getting from her men.

Her men, who ranged from Christian men to school officials to drug dealers to politicians to businessmen to lawyers—whoever could pay the bill or satisfy the moment, offered amusement throughout the years. Though she often gave them her body, she learned to protect her soul. Many of them knew little if anything about her. She, instead, had mastered techniques to get men to expose their souls. They told her secrets about themselves, their wives and children, their businesses, and she even got them to expose their insecurities. She, of course, played on that and offered them everything they lacked. If their wife was too caught up in her career, she became the listener and comforter. If the home was too stressful, she made them feel relaxed and open. What first started out to be an understanding had turned into a relationship. They had tried to impart their wisdom to her, they offered free trips and gifts, and some even said that they loved her (a couple wanted to leave their wives). But she convinced them that she was only for a season—to be there for them at this moment in their lives.

She had no shame in her deeds, for she was letting out the "woman in her." She was experiencing sexuality at its fullest and at the expense of others. She was only doing as they had done to her.

Though there were many men in and out of her life, she can only vividly remember a few. Because once it was over, she had erased most of them from her memory. They became blocked out of her mind. However, as time progressed, she forgot less and less.

Her father was a pastor preaching the Gospel of Christ and she was the typical "preacher's daughter rebelling her calling." Mom was the respected evangelist and singer in many ministries, and her grandmother was the "truth." All she heard about her grandmother were bits and pieces. The marriages, a physically abusive relationship, seeing her father get burned, an entertainer, popular parties, waitress, Sunday school teacher, dressed as though she had a million dollars, and so on. But she had never seen any of it—only heard. By the time she was born, her grandmother had vowed her mind, body, and spirit to herself. No more romantic or intimate relationships or extended visits or anything that did not involve her typical day of going to work and coming back home. She spent most of her younger years with her. And from that moment on, her grandmother's time and wisdom were important to her. She labeled her a "soul survivor"—not quite living but nowhere close to dying. They took long walks and her talks were honest.

"I never had nothing given to her and that's why I'm so hard on you. Never depend on no one, her grandmother said.

She could count the number of times she saw her grandmother cry. She had plans to adopt her strength. Sandra could see a little of herself in her grandmother. The way she'd hold things in, gather her facts, and break painful facts at the last moment. She could break and console you with your words. When Clara began to show her the truth of what had become her new reality, she made it no secret how disappointed she was in her and Clara made it no secret how much she didn't care.

Her family seemed to never miss a function, or special event or anything that mattered. Whenever she got in trouble, there they were bailing her out. Some would wonder why at times she hated them. Maybe it was her mother who never wanted her to play with the other kids, who kept her pulling her hair out about her schoolwork, or who never knew her own worth until it was almost too late. She had seen her mother give the coat off her back to people who never deserved it. She had seen her starve for attention and live in a fantasy world that she was never really part of. Her mother got all dressed up in clothes that matched her shoes and pranced with people who only wanted to take advantage of her. It was from her mother that she gained the knowledge how to love too hard too soon.

Unlike her grandmother, her mother was a secret. She was a sensitive woman with a strong heart who could save the world with her love. And here, in those days, she did not even know how to save her. It had broken her heart to even think that somewhere she had missed something so valuable in her life. Her mother's searching had never really come to an end. Searching for answers of abandonment. She was certain her mother had died a thousand deaths—from the death of her first child to the abuse of her past. Raised down south, rarely exposed to the larger world, she, too, had found out too late how harsh the city could be. Though she was determined and well educated, this did not stop her longing inside; so, she would settle for a romantic gift of gab if it seemed promising. Sandra instead lost respect for the woman who loved her so. She hoped as her mother had. Yet her mother was her confidante and they needed one another. She was the arm she could lay on when things became tough. She was the one who saved her life whenever she thought about suicide again. She was the hopeless believer when no one else believed.

Throughout the years, her callous and nonchalant behavior taught her mother not to care so much. Her ever-changing boyfriends and lack of commitment showed her mother how not to love so hard, and her blunt tongue and dry eyes told her mother that it was okay to speak her mind. So they taught each other. They learned together from each other's experiences that life was defined by love and, one way or another, it would affect your life—whether you were loving too hard or not loving at all. This was true of their relationship as well.

Maybe it was her father who never seemed to stand up because of fear. He had in many ways masked his pain with his life in the Lord. His wrongly directed emotions had too often lied. He seemed to be forever searching for the truth that he already knew. He would make decisions too late and sit in his guilt, which he carefully masked with his kindness. He loved her more than life itself and would cry and pray for whatever he could not say. She remembered the songs they shared, the churches she would sing at with him, the days he would do her hair, and wrestle with her—everything that gave them such a spiritual connection. Her father, the opposite of her mother, understood nature and the importance of the "quiet." But he feared intimacy. He even feared her breaking his heart (which she had done). He feared anything that was out of his control the way love sometimes could be. So he took her to psychiatrists and counselors and prayer warriors—anything that could fix the problem. He said she gave him high blood pressure and that he stayed on his knees because of her.

But she prayed for him. His broken family life had never been fully confronted and it had become evident in his three broken marriages. He had often called her a mystery and she had proved him right. If he had known the whole story, he wouldn't have been able to sleep. So she protected him.

It was years until her conscience started to kick in. She was 17 and living in New Jersey with a 20-year-old man who would have kissed the ground she walked on if she asked. Ronald was an intellectual. He talked, walked, and dressed "proper." A hopeless romantic as she remembered it. Bubble baths, candlelight dinners, soft music, everything to make a lady's heart melt. Except for hers. He was all man and she appreciated him. It seemed as though he had figured out what she was all about and chose to accept it anyway. So he would talk and lecture her about love and life and what he would do for her if she would "just be right." He gave her the first taste of consciousness—her first wanting to know and discover herself. Sometimes she'd try to force herself to be in love with him, but she couldn't. He had seen something in her that she didn't see.

"Girl, you are brilliant, intelligent—everything a woman should be. You have the world in your hands. You are going to be somebody someday and going to make a difference in people's lives."

"Why, because I got out of high school in three years?" she would sarcastically say.

"No, because you're special," he would reply. "I can see it in your eyes."

"In my eyes," she would think.

"My eyes lie," she would reply with no explanation.

Too often she was laughing only not to remember. Too often she had crafted the perfect words, and dressed in her Sunday clothes. She had painted her smile and wore contacts to hide. Can't he see the pain? She was the rapist's dream, the pervert's target. She couldn't love if it shot her. And if it did catch her, she would probably die from its sting.

Ronald was a hard-working young man raised in group homes. He fought the system so that he would not become a statistic. He was willing to work two jobs to put her through school, but she had merely admired him. He'd soon find out when she came home with the hickey on her neck. When he kicked her out, she realized how much he cared.

Tubo was as eccentric as his name. He was a dedicated, hard-working man who captured her heart during their conversations on the stoop and walks in the park. Even his silence was golden. Though she often told him lies, she loved talking to him. He was a breath of fresh air. Something new and different. His demeanor and thuggish qualities attracted her to him. She was pleased by the way he dressed, his intelligence, his motivation. She was in for a long ride.

Days went quickly and the nights did not feel that cold. He warmed her to a deeper consciousness—one unlike any other she had experienced. She smiled wider and laughed harder when she was with him. She even closed her eyes when he made love to her. She wanted to feel every inch of him. For the first time, she wanted to feel pure. He told her he loved her, and she loved him, too. But her body longed for another's touch. A touch like something she had felt before. She would creep out on him when things got too tough. Back to those married and older men; that was fulfilling that need. She had a soul tie with them. A soul tie that would not let her let them go. Her lies were as confusing as her love.

Tubo would soon find out—he was too street smart not to. She had not yet considered his feelings but was concerned only with her own desires. It wasn't even their sex that made the others so desirable. It was the way they all held her a little differently. The way each one looked and touched her in different places. It was the conversation and little pieces of memory each one had given her. But it was still magic, the way Tubo and she clicked. The way they melted into each other. Yet no matter how hard she tried, she could not run away from the others. She had adored him, but not enough. His temper was his only flaw—the way he would torture her with his tongue. So when he found out, he threw every secret back at her. He felt betrayed.

When he found out who she was and what she was doing, he beat her. He beat her so bad that she had a broken eardrum and severe contusions. He flared at the woman to whom he had given his heart, who had the audacity to not be honest with him. It reminded him of the abusive mother who never really showed him love. He, like her, was different and had been denied the joys of being a child. They had shared each other's pain and looked for comfort in each other. Now they had come to the point of ultimate betrayal.

She dropped all of the charges. She claimed that she understood. She felt as though she deserved it in one way or another and vowed to never be the same. Unsuccessfully, she tried to show him her attempt to change, but never enough to let the others go. So he let her go. She had never been let go before.

She had loved him to the extent that she could, and he abandoned her and threw her back to the wolves again. She could not eat or sleep, and she lost her breath. Her college roommates did routine suicide watches. She was dying emotionally. Not going to classes—"A zombie" was what that other students called her, the contemporary <u>Sula</u>. Some could not believe she had let someone slip into her soul.

"Girl, you got to snap out of it," she heard them say.

They couldn't understand why she was so hurt when she was doing so wrong. She said it was because he was everything to her, that he meant more than sex.

So she packed up and went to a place where she could hear only the birds chirp to finish her college years. Everyone could tell she had experienced a loss. She began writing to keep her soul from dying. The professors claimed "lack of passion and anger." But she said she had not awakened yet. Her senses had failed her for the first time.

One unborn baby later she was loving him again. It had been a year and some and she was still putty in his arms. She had matured to new rules of life—no more married men. He came along with temporary fulfillment. She could remember the smile from the moment they met again. She moved in with him and they loved as though love were going out of style. She would proudly make his food, wash his clothes, and walk down the street with him hand in hand. She got branded with his street name—it represented his ownership and power over her. She bragged about the engagement ring he bought and the love they made. They vacationed in Cancun while he stole her freedom.

She hid secrets of the cyst that always appeared on her vagina, and hid the other health problems, too. It was only three weeks before they had officially gotten back together that she learned about her cancer. It had an affect on her body. She bled four months straight while she was with him. He made her feel as though the cancer was a result of her lifestyle. Though he cried, he claimed that God was punishing her for her promiscuity. It was with him that she learned how to scream and cry like a newborn child forced into a cold, cold world.

During chemotherapy, she never saw him. She couldn't figure out how she could go from being so strong to ending up so helpless. Some days, she needed help to the bathroom. Other days, she couldn't find the strength to cry, but she had to fight for her life. She watched her hair fall and face grow older. She prayed and talked to God more than she ever had. It was all she could do. Sometimes she'd just sit and recollect things she had forgotten or not wanted to recall; she'd just look in the mirror and analyze her life.

It wasn't until the end of her senior year that she had finally completed all of her therapy. It taught her how to be alone. She learned peace.

It was "Milk," her girlfriend, who really showed her who she was. It was Milk's love and dedication that kept her from dying before her time. Milk's lifestyle was an example. The reading of the Bible, trips to the Mosque, inspirational lectures, and everything positive that reminded her of her worth. Milk was sent to her from God. An angel, she might say. Milk read her mind, understood her, and loved her.

The quietness had been her escape for much too long and she was ready to return to the same life with a different lifestyle. She had been so into herself that by the time she looked up, it had been six months since she had been touched.

Back in New York, she could write again. She could look the same men in the eyes and not desire them anymore. One day, she looked at Tubo and he did not look the same. She got out of his black Toyota Camry and ran. She ran so fast that her knees gave out on her. She ran until she was able to feel what freedom felt like. He had taken so much from her and it seemed that the harder she ran, the more of herself she snatched back. She was running and crying as though her life depended on it. It did.

She wondered when the healing would ever manifest itself. When was it safe to love again? She had a heart of bruises and a soul of stone. Not even a bullet could make her fall to her knees. Loving again, crying again would be hard.

Bulletproof Souls- Part 2

I am suffering from the men that I let attach their souls
to me
Then snatch their soul away
I know they must have some joy that they give to their
new lady
Some more pep to their step
With wisdom and compassion
Some serious love to share

There are children I never had for them
While I practiced being humble
I let them have possession of my body
And control a piece of my mind
Now I see them with their happy endings
And laugh at my ancient thought that I was in total
control
And Queen of my throne

I took interest in their desires
While they suppressed mine
I said that respect would come when their potential
blossomed
If I only gave it a little time
Time that turned into deserted lands

And I became the honeycomb deprived of natural
juices
I, the maiden, became the rose wilted by the Son
I became the spirit extinct
The soul vested

What you gonna do?

Not with your body or overrated sex
Your size two tank
Or the way your tongue ring clicks
But it's the wisdom from the tongue that will kill them
Ladies
It's the mind that will earn you respect
That will make them look at you differently

For many cannot see
Stains on abstract cotton sheets
Or bruises of the brick-covered lambs
They don't care about the pains that made you scared
To commit or forget
Everything that made you into that hoe or bitch

Those painted porcelain masks will not hold up forever
One day they too shall see you cry
Those lies won't stand with you for long, my sisters,
For you will soon wear, eat, and sleep the truth
'Cause one day that makeup is going to smear
And that dress ain't gonna fit right no more
That hair will turn a burnt gray and those bedroom eyes
will fall

What you gonna do when they come for you, my sister?
When they come to take you home?
What you gonna say on judgment day?
That you've made the world your home
That all your desires and accomplishments are mixed
up in these material things

That all you possess goes no further than what they've
already seen

I say, it's not in what you show them that make them
value you
But in the quiet intangible things

Inform them of your successes
Let your character expose their emptiness
Destroy them with His love and everything great He's
done for you
Let them hear your eloquence shaped by your
worthiness
Instead of giving up your preciousness

It's not his dollars, ladies, that determine his manliness
But it's in his look
It's his unselfish touch
The intelligent beauty he can pull out of you
Not by the quickness of his tongue
But by how many times he makes you think without
taking off your clothes
The way he takes your hand when you are afraid
How he invests in the future that he sees
Not in your worldliness
Or kisses from Delilah's nest

It's not in all the different experiences that made you a
groupie superstar
'Cause one day them curls gonna become loose
And that overpermed hair ain't gonna look pretty no
more

Black Dresses Stain

That tongue gonna become s-l-o-w
And those teeth gonna rot
Those breasts gonna hang
As low as your head

What you gonna do when they come for you, my sister?
When they come to take you home?
What you gonna say on judgment day?
That you've made the world your home
That all your desires and accomplishments are mixed
up in these material things
That all you possess goes no further than what they've
already seen

A Soldier's Story

He said that I would live again because of his sex
That he never had to mention love
He could have me wide open with his lips
I would fall into the texture of his sheets
While his fingers dug into the center of my heart
With his dirty hands

He said that God may have the whole world in his
hands
But he had me in the will of his sex
That I couldn't be angry with the desires of my heart
Because my mind always wandered back to love
While he just fantasized me in between his sheets
Shocking me with his lips

He said that it was easy for lies to come from the lips
And even more clever if it was followed by the hands
As he told me the stories of his sheets
I pondered the graciousness of his sex
And dreamed of the mystery of his wonderful love
When he was a soldier with his heart

He said that true pain derives from the heart
But would never be told from his lips
Because he never was taught to believe in love
Yet his ultimate faith lied in his hands
Or in the positioning of his sex
His secrets were discovered through the sheets

He said that language derived from his crispy clean
sheets
And my misfortune had mistaken it for my heart
That life's gain originated from the beauty of sex
Never involving the kissing of lips
Only emotion in the movement of hands
And that was the definition of his love

I told him that I did not give a fuck about his love
Because I knew what lied beneath the pattern of his
sheets
And the empty motion of his hands
That my power protected my heart
And for the moment I controlled him with my lips
As I covered up my lies with my sex

When he said that love equaled bullshit only to be mea-
sured by the sex
I buried my lips in his hands
As the sheets told the tale of my heart

Moments In Time

This Muslim guy
Talked of undeniable respect
For the Black woman
He dabbled words of manhood
And spit pictures of fantasies
He proclaimed true intention
Of knowing how to treat this Nubian Queen
He spoke of the permanence of his caress
And stroked my desires
He teased unspoken insecurities with his lies

He laid me down on his cold wrinkle sheets
And screwed me with a smile
He faked love with a willing heart
Ten minutes of intensity had taught me his thoughts
His eyes pierced this familiarity
He left me wrapped in winter rain
Robotically
His mind dressed me with the word goodbye
Before the night had closed its eyes
As my tears hit the bus floor
I could hear him reciting the Quran

A fine Christian brother once said
"I love the Lord with all my heart"
Ran down the scriptures like the devil he was
I was flabbergasted by his wisdom
And overstanding knowledge of something so sacred to
my heart
"He the one," I said.

"The one who could love me because he loved God first"
He waited three long weeks
All the while confessing his sins
The blessing of forgiveness
The commitment to his church body and its leaders
He spoke of the importance of a holy life
And righteous upbringing
The value of truth
"Because the truth had set him free"
Free enough to release the clothing off my back
He flowed through my body seductively
Corrupting our temples
He held me overnight
Before he forsake me

Because I believed they were representatives of God
I chose one that never spoke religion
And he lasted longer than the few
His seduction and agape love seemed eternal
With no fancy words to give
Even when the sex wasn't heavenly
This one loved me in return for mine
The one that I can't forget
Only spoke of forever
Yet ended too soon

Marked

"A Black woman with cancer!" she couldn't fathom it. It had taken away her youth and was eating away at her body like locusts. It was like nothing she had experienced. She called it the "slow death." She credited it to her loose, carefree life, but mostly claimed it had come from a series of broken hearts. She told the doctors that no medicine could heal her type of pain. That she was "girl interrupted."

She saw her breasts fall, bags deepen under her eyes, and figure change into that of a sloppy rag doll. She was in too much pain to cry and had too little energy to speak. She just observed and thought about all the little things that she thought mattered when she was healthy. "If I ever come out alive, it'll be different," she promised. She promised to reserve her heart for herself and her mind for her own. She would never sacrifice her soul again. She vowed to deal with this alone so that it may help her grow.

Lying down, she remembered the unpleasant things, the pleasant things, the forgotten things. She remembered her daddy's kisses, her mother's smile, her grandmother's words. She remembered every man she had ever lain with and what they took with them when they left (because they all had taken something). She remembered abuses, love, and the one rose that grew in her backyard when she was a baby.

She couldn't swallow pills—but had to now. She loved her long hair—but lost all of it. She thought couldn't live without sex—but had not experienced a touch in months. Though she had lost what she had thought was her strength, she was the strongest she had ever been. "In all this loss," she claimed, "I will rediscover myself."

But rediscovering herself was something she did not yet know how to do. Was she to travel down memory lane and heal herself? And if she did, would it bring her joy back? Was she to give up all earthly treasures and things of this world to become a new spiritual being on a new spiritual path? And if she did, would God finally answer her? Was she to adopt this suddenly imposed life of celibacy? And if she did, would all other desires be snatched away with it? How this life had deceived her.

Other people always saw her as being strong but now she couldn't even pretend. Yet pretending is something she had done so well. Before the cancer, she pretended that everything was okay. That she was a millennium girl stuck in a hippie body—so her desires were free and smooth—and she could fly if she wanted to. She pretended that her middle-class family was actually paying for her college tuition and that she was borderline rich. She pretended that those who came and went had not had an impact on her—that the breaking had made her stronger. She pretended that she actually liked people and loved herself.

The truth was, she had never sat still long enough to find out who she was and wasn't ever interested in herself. Never quite a straight-A student, but bright enough to get skipped. Never really athletic or creative but loving the art of both. Never gorgeous but a median of pretty and cute. Never agreeing, never fully intimate, never belonging, and never really there—anywhere. She was always somewhere in between or nowhere at all. She could feel it—when her friends got high and they passed the blunt by her, when she'd go to study groups and realize how shallow the brilliant people were, when Black people looked too ghetto, the white ones too privileged, and Spanish too confused. She embraced everything without making a decision on anything or anyone.

She said that at least now, with the emergence of her cancer, she could relax. Relax in whatever would become of the situation—an untimely death or new life. She didn't mind the way people were acting now—as if she were never alive before. She didn't care if they talked about her. Or if the same guys who had fucked her and ate her out took disgust in the reshaping of her body or her sudden sickness that uncontrollably showed up in the middle of class. She knew her strength had failed her and that no one was around to catch her anymore. Not that anyone was around from the beginning but, at least, they had pretended, too.

She hated the silence—the times when she could spend time only with herself and her energy was below zero. She hated the dark, so she always kept the lights on. She hated the moments when the phone was too far away or the next door neighbors didn't fight or when she forgot to leave the radio or television on or when the nurse didn't send someone over to see whether she ate dinner that night or when her feet were too cold and she was thinking about how she was going to make it to the bathroom. And somehow, some way, she always seemed to get a meal and make it to the bathroom just in time.

The shedding of her hair seemed to be the fall of her glory. It was the first time she could remember feeling bad about her situation. Her thick, black, long hair was falling out into the sink and thinning quickly. So she just cut it all off and, in doing this, she mourned silently. She didn't know whether she was mourning the loss of her hair or the loss of her glory. The two seemed so connected. Her hair was a part of her beauty—the part of herself that she used to entice her men. Now both had been violently snatched and seemingly without any adequate fight.

How could you fight something you couldn't control?! She had always been in control. She carefully mapped out her career, her men, her future plans—and even when they'd drift from time to time, the end result was always the way she expected. It was no surprise when she got out of high school and college in three years or when Johnny had finally gotten over her or when she had finally got over Kenneth after all those years. Nothing came as a surprise anymore—except for this—and she felt as though a weak man had just beaten her up. She had just gotten bamboozled from Venus— the Love goddess—and God had placed a stamp on her face marked PUNISHED while throwing a surprise party in her honor.

And she dreamed, and wondered, and thought…about why she needed the quiet. Why the loneliness was now her healing, and the silence was her deadly friend that she hated to love and wanted to hate. I can't tell you why she ran away from them for so long when she should have embraced it. I watched her and cried for her. I stood proxy for the revival of her spirit— even before the cancer came. Before the cancer, he was her cancer.

He wanted to touch her but I knew that she could

never be really touched. Because even though she covered the tattoo, the scar remained. She, marked in deep black ink, revealed the stories of herself when she was loving freely, simply, effortlessly—when it was all about her. Then, back then, I admired the way she smiled as though it was a gift and laughed as though it were a song and gave herself away so easily. I don't know how and when it became about him. But whenever she'd talk about him, I'd see Buddha in her eyes. She quoted him like he was the author of the Scriptures. She said when he'd touch her she was paralyzed and revived at the same time. He had her even further than where she had already been—on a planet called "them," where he was the only one that mattered.

She drifted away from me. There were moments when I would see her and she was awaiting, praying for, and idolizing his call. But I'd remind her of her nature. And so, to please me, she'd unfoolishly let the others feel her because I knew she liked to be felt. Then, with tears in her eyes, she'd tell me that no one could touch her like him. So I wanted to know how he had managed to steal the best from her—how he had dethroned her—how he had remolded her mind. She said that even before the tattoo, he had looked her in her eyes and asked to see the things that had marked her. So she had given him the key to her secret place.

"I cut my finger and bled for him. I let him hang me over his balcony. I used his toothbrush. I briefed him on our love every morning from the corner of his tub even when I knew there were mice in there. He was introduced to all my VIPs and Lever 2000 parts- even when the parts were still bleeding," she later told me.

I never let her say that she was "dying" but he never came to see her while she was waiting to die. Though we acted as though he never existed, it didn't take much to see that she was suffering from what she thought was a tragedy and from what I thought was a new beginning. I never let her talk about her pain around me. I'd only remind her of the strong diva she was to be. So when she finally went through recovery, we acted as though those years were forgotten.

When she had mastered the wigs and the men again, we'd laugh about how they had fallen in love with her contacts and fake hair.

Once she said, "Thank you for saving me when I was dying and when he…"

"Girl, I don't even remember that," I replied, " I only remember you as strong, as queen."

"As queen!" she laughed. "Well, one thing is for sure, the memory might fail but the marks never do."

Big Toe

Tears from overdeveloped eyes
Fall into an hourglass
Of melted memories
Onto paved cemented streets
That yearn for air

She calls out to the clouds
Raining on city umbrellas

Black Ones
Keeping the people awake
In constant pain
Because life is moving past them

He won't pick up his pants
Because they represent life
Defined by his 4 by 6 room
Where blood stains are underneath blue paint
The same color as his jeans
The same as his dog's collar
Who won't let him touch her
Cause he's mean

She suppresses her screams
To a laugh
To a compromise
To a "yes"
Through her child-bearing of the world

Those white shoes

Don't dance like they use to
And that big toe is holding down all of the others

Faded Senses
He as My Identity

He smelled like JOOP in the '90s and Salvatore Ferragamo in the new century. I never forgot his smell. I almost grabbed the man in the dark green coat, smothered the Italian man on the empty C train, and became a lesbian when the woman in the jeans smiled at me. I spent too much time in the cologne department in Macy's or Saks or Lord and Taylor's searching for him. Sometimes I would leave the Chinese restaurant in his neighborhood and swear I'd just missed him.

It wasn't as though I needed to see him anyway. He would have just messed with my mind. But I couldn't forget his smell. I remembered the train platform he'd walk me to at 3 o'clock in the morning before he got his car. The times he'd dare me to have sex in the train car…and I almost did. The looks he'd give me—good or bad—on the days when we tried to figure out each other. The seasons changed as the years passed and we moved from the shuttle and 2 and 3 trains to the 4 and 5.

I can't forget the smell of his hallway. The hallway he had before he got his own place. We slept—summer or winter—in the hallway just to be together. We fucked—standing up—holding on tight—through some semi-sheer drapes—in the night behind the red door in the hallway. Up the red stairs, past the hallway, was the entrance to his small bedroom where we'd sneak to make love. Down the red stairs, below the hallway, is where we declared our love and I lied about my history to keep him. And the hallway was our comfort zone. Then we moved from the hallway to almost no hallway at all. We transcended from privacy to a complex situation—where other people were always around.

Can I tell you about the smell of his bedroom—before his name was on it—that he said always smelled like me? But I never recognized my own scent. Instead, I would sniff and lay under his small neck. There we explored our intensity and oneness. And I would be lost in his body odor. Then, without warning, he would taste me. And when he tasted me, he ate me like he'd smell the way I did. That's how I reassured myself of his love for me.

Just when I became full of his smell, he moved from a small room to an extra-large one where his scent became lost in the air. The space interrupted the proximity of his touch. When he'd touch me, the touch was too far apart for me to feel it. I even tried to rearrange the room but he'd always change it back.

Then he lost my scent and forgot the smell of his old hallway. He did not look at me the same anymore. He did not call my name the way he used to. He became too busy to read my poems and discuss my writings. Then I found out that he had already started a family. That everything I had invested and endured was already given away.

If I could go back, I would have never gotten out of that Toyota Camry. I would never give him back any-thing for everything he took away from me. I would have found out where she lived, gone there, and made her feel what I felt all those years I spent with him. I would have told her that she could not have him because I had given him my soul. I would have taken him to court for girl-friend alimony—for every tear he could not see.

He told me that I should stay alive because Lauryn Hill was coming out with another CD, and I did. It had been five years and I still could hear his voice. I regretted that we didn't share the "Jay-Z and Friends," Badu's "Underground Village," and Scott's "Beautifully Human" together. There were songs, thoughts, and moments that reminded me of us.

On my way from my second job, I walked past his house at least twice a week. I gained a little weight from the baby (that I had for another man) and prayed that I never stumbled into his by the woman he cheated on me with. I prayed that he never ran into me and asked about the family (that wasn't) or my life (that he helped to break). I had rehearsed my smile and script at least a thousand times in preparation of his presence. Maybe too many times—but I knew he wasn't worth a knock on the door or my ringing his bell. All I knew is that whatever was said had to be on time and perfect because he would be winning again if it wasn't.

I said that it was part of the healing process that I had been brought back to the place that had defined pain and identified strength for me. Sometimes I wouldn't look around—afraid that his face was too close. It was a mystery how attached I was to him. How we became bread and butter, glove and hand, and he the foundation on which I stood.

I pushed the dream that had already been there and he pushed the "other" woman out of me. First I was "freak," then I was "humble," then he taught me how to scream like I was a "street girl" with no home-training. He stuck the "streets" inside of me. So when my college roommates began to call me crazy (when I had those moments of withdrawal), I knew that he had the best of me. Those years I tried to reach deep to grab "me" back were lost in him. Even when we were apart, I carried the experience of us. The withdrawal was stronger than a drug because he hid my spirit from me—he spit on my soul.

It was with time and space that I had to teach myself to be refined again. Before him, I must have been eye candy to all men. But after, it seemed as though I had passed my peak. Before him, I could time how quickly they'd fall in love. But after, they were loving and leaving.

Many moments, I questioned how I let him get the most of me. But the answer was never quite clear. He wasn't too good-looking or overly –intelligent, but he had mastered how to control my mind and body. I believed his words, intentions, and motives. I trusted him as though he was God.

Our best times were spent in poverty. Before I had the college degree and he the car—when I would sleep with him in the hallway of his mother's house—he treated me as if were precious. And I thought he was sent to save my life—to protect me. Whenever we would separate and come back together again, his sex got better, words got stronger, and I became more serious about my monogamy.

Near the end, I heard rumors of the other women but I couldn't accept that he would be disloyal to me. And I owed him all of my loyalty. So I let him pick me up at one, two, and three o'clock in the morning every night after he finished "his business." I let him tell me to take a cab because he didn't want to lose his parking space. I bitterly bit my tongue when I knew he wasn't answering his cell phone for a reason. I let him win all those petty arguments he started—just to keep the peace and hope that we were still in love. And though I came home to him every night and wore his diamond ring, I waited for him to open the door for me since he never offered me the key.

The last day we were together as a couple was a Sunday morning. We went to the afternoon church service and I heard the inaudible loud voice saying, "It's time to let go." I knew our years had been built on lies. That when I was lying, he wasn't and when I didn't, he did. When I wasn't faithful, he was and when I was, he wasn't.

With his being four years my senior, I tried to tell him that he couldn't take on an abused 17-year-old girl and turn her into a real woman. By the time 21 came around, my experiences had made me different and I was ready to be the woman he wanted. Then his wants changed and he began to need more from me—needs I blame on insecurity. It was not long before I figured out that we had passionately loved and hated—wanted and despised—become each other's worst enemy and most valuable player.

I had just wanted him to say that the years were too strong or friendship and secrets too deep or too many tears have been shed to just walk away as if we never existed. That our senses belonged to one another.

We knew that keeping doors open was too dangerous. So I looked back but without him knowing. Though this separation proved to be final, I had to heal from those years of loving him.

X

I had called him one true love
And he called me X
He had X'ed me out of the picture for her
And I was trying to X him out of my heart
My mind had unconsciously meandered to places that
reminded me of we
We had set a legacy of love
That had become a part of this Generation X
I had cuts on my neck that reminded me of him
And he had the bruises of the heart
I had him written on the calendars of my future
And he had me on the Black book of his past

I couldn't forget how X-quisite it was when he touched me
And he
How X-cellent it was when I left
So easily he had X-ed me out of his memory
And for so long I could not release
I pondered on the X's O's and love that was made with-
out intercourse

Sometimes I had to shiver to purge the semen he had
left inside of me years ago
I'd have the shakes when I smelt his cologne on another
man
I had remembered him too fondly

He was the reason I had run away
The New York streets had too purely pricked my mind
It was him in Newark, Philly, and Eastern Parkway

It was he that scared me so much
I had run away to X-scape
The love and pain he had made me accountable for

Coming back, had stroked his ego
To know that a million men had never taken his place
I'm sure he had shared a laugh or two
At the foolish me
Who loved him still

My girlfriend said I was too X-ceptional to settle for an
emotional second
But I told her
It was just to hear him breathe
To feel his hand
Again
That I was staying true to me

How could something so rare just past my eyes and slip
through my fingers
How could this woman take my X-position and become
what I was
Who I am
Where I belong
How could she replace that X-rated history of when he
was loving me
Deeper than he ever had
Stronger than he'd ever known
Soulmates is what he called we
A word that she didn't deserve
A phrase she could not yet have earned

It was unhealthy the way I had loved and hated him
In my intensity
Anger
Unfaithfulness
Passion
I had loved him still
The same
Even as his X

The Way the Wind Blows

It was before dinner and she, with all the strength she had left, walked into the woods as far and as fast as she could. Finally, she collapsed right under the tree shaken and torn by the hurricane. Staring at the ivy leaf that had finally rusted and fallen off the tree, her stomach felt as though someone was tearing her uterus out of her. She knew this would happen. The woman told her so. She gathered all the leaves that were in arm's reach, lifted up her tiny torso, and slid them under her. She delicately pushed up her dress and watched the leaves turn red. Then she closed her eyes and let the wind seep in between her thighs. She thought how good the wind felt on her body. The city could never offer her this. She cherished the moments when she could see only the trees blow and hear the birds chirp.

"Sharon!

"Sharon, girl, where are you?"

"Sharon, you better answer me if you out there!"

She scurried to cover the leaves with fresh ones as she answered, "I'm coming, ma'am."

With each step, she practiced straightening out her walk until she had perfected it by the time she reached the house.

"Sharon, what did I tell you about going into those woods by yourself. Anything could be out there. You know how many dirty men lurk in the woods waiting for a pretty little thing like you. Next time take Junior with you."

"Yes, ma'am. It's just that Junior is so busy studyin' and all."

"I know, child. I'm so proud of my baby. He gonna be a college man next year wit a full scholarship—an academic one at that. Lord knows I wish I had half the brains you kids have. Then, I wouldn't have to work three jobs just to make ends meet. Sharon, that gonna be you in a couple years. You gonna be a college woman and yo mama would be so proud."

Her mother, Isabella Williams, taught her all she knew about life. Sharon would call her Isabella because her mother hated it when Sharon called her "ma" or "mommy." She said it made her feel too old. Isabella loved the city. She hated the South and didn't want to visit her old home for anything, even for the funeral of her mother. She said that all the South was good for was secrets and people pretending to be something that they are not.

"Sharon, baby, you can do whatever you want in life, as long as you are smart. Not only in the classroom but life," Isabella would always say. "Life is something you gotta study like a maze in order to escape. Otherwise, the maze will just drive you crazy."

She believed in all the unconventional things, such as how a man wasn't needed to raise a baby and about talking to Sharon openly about sex. She even faked a college transcript to land an executive job in order to afford the Eastside apartment they lived in. She was a natural at getting her way and talking herself out of or into any situation.

All Sharon could remember was her mother's pale, dead, naked body on the balcony of their apartment. It was 95 degrees, and living without air conditioner caused her mother to have an asthma attack. Sharon always had to remind Isabella to take care of the things that mattered the most first—such as paying the electric bill or picking up her asthma medication—before going on a date or buying a pair of Gucci shoes. Isabella said, "life was only worth living once, so live it up" and that was her motto. Though Sharon knew how careless her mother was, Isabella's death shocked her. And if that was not of enough a surprise, Sharon's inheritance totaled $152.38 in the bank. The coroner called her death "lack of wind." Sharon said her mother's mouth was the wind.

"I know, Aunt Lilly, she sure would. She always said I was smart and savvy."

"Yeah, you sure are. If you could keep your head off of those boys. Even though I will admit that Charles does come from a nice family. He sho can give us a penny or two."

"Yeah, he's alright, but I don't need his penny," Sharon replied. "I'm gonna make my own."

"Oh, yeah. Well, you young girls always think you got it goin' on—betta take a man's help when he offers, child. How many days I wish Junior's father would come back…"

"Maybe it's time I take a bath and get ready for dinner," Sharon interrupted.

Sharon hated when her aunt started that pathetic "I wish I had someone" and "Junior is all I have" conversations.

She rushed into the house. Now that her aunt was out of her sight, Sharon could tend to her weak knees and spinning headache. She stopped to maintain her balance as she slowly made her way up the stairs to the bathroom.

"Hey, what's wrong with you?" Junior asked, spotting her outside his bedroom door.

"Nothing, Junior," Sharon replied with annoyance, "I'm not feeling so good, so stay out of my way."

"Ohh, that poor baby! What do you girls call that thing you get every month? ... A period! Must be that time of the month," he joked.

"Shut up, Junior! Don't you have a book to read or some nerdy experiment to do?"

"Nope, not really," he said blocking the bathroom. "I guess this means no kissy-kissy with Charles tonight."

"Junior, will you close your damn mouth before Aunt Lilly hears you," Sharon angrily replied.

Noticing her pain, Junior moved out of the way as Sharon slammed the bathroom door behind her. She wondered how Junior had become so immature. She was 14 and he was 17 and she had taught him things he should have already known—such as where babies come from, how to talk to a girl, and how to fight back and stand up for himself. She called him "church boy" when he made her mad because she believed that before she came there he had never committed a sin in his life.

He never had any friends before Lilly made him popular in school. Neighbors whispered that Junior was still sucking his mother's breast at seven years of age and every now and then he would still sneak in her bed. Junior could do no wrong in Aunt Lilly's eyes. If he got upset and threw a tantrum, it was because he wasn't feeling good. If Aunt Lilly couldn't afford something and he wanted it, he would convince her to work an overnight shift to earn the money. When Aunt Lilly caught the flu and Junior needed extra money for some science project, he screamed and complained so much that Aunt Lilly went to work until she almost died from pneumonia. He couldn't wash a dish, cook a dish, iron his clothes, and barely wiped his own ass well enough.

Sharon stared in the bathroom mirror and thought about her mother. She missed her so much. Isabella was always so bold and strong and fearless. Though the city had given Sharon some of the same characteristics, she found that the South had done the opposite. Just as she felt herself about to cry, she heard Junior call her.

"What, Junior?!"

"It's Charles!"

With all of her strength, Sharon hurried to the phone.

"Hello, Charles?"

"Hey, baby, how are you feelin'?"

"Not so well. Maybe we shouldn't do it anymore. I mean…" Sharon stopped when she realized that Junior was engrossed in her conversation. Then she pulled the phone in her room and slammed her bedroom door.

"It's just that I am so confused," Sharon continued.

"What do you mean? You know I love you."

"No, you don't. We too young to love. I don't love nobody."

"Sharon, from the first day you went to Bernard High I knew I loved you. I know I'm only 16 but I could be with anybody in Georgia. You the only one I want. You done taught me so much. We have so much fun together. Plus you my first and I'm yours. We could spend the rest of our lives together. I understand you said we too young to have a baby now but I could take care of you. You won't even have to work."

"Oh, hush up, Charles. You don't know what you're talking about. The truth is you ain't my first and you ain't gonna be my last." Sharon hung up the phone and cried. She cried so hard that she felt as though her head was about to explode. The phone rang but she ignored it. She wanted to go outside, but she knew Aunt Lilly wouldn't let her.

"Baby, you alright in there?" she heard Aunt Lilly ask through the door,

"Yeah, I'm okay, auntie. Just that time of the month. I'm feelin a little crampy. Do you mind if I skip dinner tonight? I'm not feelin' hungry," she answered.

"Are you sure? I could always bring you a plate."

"No, I'm okay. Thanks."

"Well, I'll leave one in the refrigerator just in case you get hungry later."

She heard Aunt Lilly walk down the stairs to begin the daily conversation with Junior about his needs, wants, desires, and overall happiness. She wanted to just close her eyes and dream.

By the time Sharon woke up, it was 10 p.m. at a cool 75 degrees. She was just thinking how good it felt that she had not been disturbed when she heard her door creak open.

"Sharon!"

"What, Junior?! Where is Aunt Lilly?"

"She's at work," Junior replied.

"Not tonight, Junior."

"Why not! Is it as heavy as before?"

"Worse. Much worse," Sharon answered.

"Let me see," Junior demanded as he rushed to pull down her pants. She tried to fight but his body was far stronger than his mind. So she finally gave in. While he was taking off his shirt and pants, she was remembering how it all started.

It was 70 degrees after the rain on Sunday. She and Charles had been planning it for months. They even bought a book about it and read it together. This afternoon around 4 p.m., they went into the woods and she found what she called "the perfect tree." She pressed her small back against the trunk of the tree as he lifted her up. They kissed as her hands unbuttoned his pants. He moaned when she touched it. She thought that maybe she tinkled when she realized that her panties were wet, but then remembered what her mother told her would happen when a woman gets aroused. She loved Charles. Everything about him. She knew he adored her. His pants dropped to his ankles and he laid her down on the wet leaves. He kneeled beside her and began playing with her breasts and kissing them softly as she sighed with delight.

How wonderful it felt! He kissed her clitoris. (He learned it from the book.) She shriveled and arched her back in pleasure. Then he took off his pants and lay beside her.

"Are you sure we are ready?" Charles asked.

"Yes," she answered. "I love you."

"I love you, too."

He climbed on top of her and gently pressed until pain became pleasure and her fingerprints became scratches on his body. Her silent screams turned into longing moans. He didn't know how to control it—this feeling. He shook almost violently and she lay underneath him for almost an hour—he still inside of her—as the wind caressed her thighs.

She was conscious again. She began to realize that it was past her curfew when they jumped up and put on their clothes. Charles kissed her goodbye before he walked home. She was putting on her last piece when she spotted movement. It was him. He had caught her. And his facial expression was as if he had experienced the pleasure himself.

"Sharon, do you hear me? What the hell is that on your clothes? You never showed me anything like that before! Why is it all over the place? You even got some on the sheets!!" Junior panicked." Are you dying or something?"

"I told you it was bad tonight, Junior."

"Yeah, well you've lied before. Bet you would never lie to Charles like that."

"Leave him out of this, Junior."

"Bet you he get some whenever he want. And how come you don't do those sounds with me like you were making with him. I saw how you were all over him…what, I ain't good enough?"

"Junior, please!"

Just as she screamed, lightning struck outside. Junior was frightened. The storm that was promised had come. He put on his clothes and silently went into his bedroom and closed the door. It was the first time he had closed his bedroom door in months, so she knew it was okay to close hers. So she went to her door quietly closed it and locked it.

"Tonight will be my first night of peace," she thought.

As the storm became louder, she pondered on

Charles—how she had lied to him. On killing Junior's baby. On her mother. She opened the two windows, lay down on the bed, opened her legs wide, and let the wind speak.

"Tomorrow will be different," she promised.

Winter

This night it snowed more than it ever had this time of the year. It was a cold snow, not like the other fair-weather snow that children could play in. Icicles fell from the building, almost apologetic for the nights that were too peaceful. He had always come in late but tonight he was especially early. Tonight was the night. He was ready to tell her how he felt, to proclaim his true intention, to uncover his mask, unleash his heart, and caress her secrets. He'd shaken off his boots of hard work and snow and strategically placed them in the closet. The darkness covered the room and for some reason he didn't disturb it. He was used to it. He could deal with the silence as long as it wasn't too painful. In the distance he could hear water running from the faucet.

"Baby, why are you in the dark with the water on?"

He turned on the light but it was just her usual untidy, forgetful ways that always drove him crazy. Today it did not bother him; as a matter of- fact, he smiled. He couldn't wait to tell her about his future plans, his dreams, his day at work, or the phone call his mother had given him today for the first time in years. He finally felt free. Tears seeped from the corners of his eyes (both of joy and pain) letting him know he could love again. For so long he had been running from the world, and it had affected her. When failures seemed to be his fate, he had lost a sense of his confidence, self-esteem, and most important, trust. He fought with his emotions. Every time he felt his heart slip, even a little bit, he'd catch it and tuck it back in—as though he meant to keep it for himself. His complexity, he felt, made him special. He was right. This loner chose his life and few friends carefully. It had even seemed as though he had handpicked his family. His clothes were unique and particularly decorated to match his mood. He shared what he wanted and packed the rest in a tight suitcase in the closet and threw away the key.

He quietly crept into the bedroom to give her a kiss in the middle of her dreams. Instead he found wrinkled sheets, as though they had gone through a turbulence of a distressing night of decisions.

"She can't be at work. She had off tonight… Maybe she's doing overtime."

Something must have happened, he thought. He began to recognize the arrival of his newfound concern.

He surprised himself. He wanted to wrap his arms around her and never let go. To tell her how much he appreciated her. Maybe even shed a tear. "Nah," he laughed. He wasn't going to give her too much just yet.

"What do you mean she's not there? Okay, thanks."

No note on the bed. In the bathroom, nothing. Closet was empty. She was gone.

His eyes were stoned to the white kitchen walls as they echoed her words last night.

"Why one more failure? Why one more goodbye? Don't you want us to work out? Let's prove the world wrong and show that love does still exist. We can sacrifice our feelings sometimes, can't we? Aren't we worth each other's best? Can't we make love and make it last forever? Why prostitute ourselves for someone else who might not even care? Show me you need me and want me, can't you? We can be like the movies, the songs. We can live the fantasies, can't we? Be my soulmate. Show me you care sometimes?" she begged.

"I am trying. Damn, I'm never enough for you. Am I?! This is me! Accept it or leave," he replied.

She did. She was tired of fighting and he was her last resort. Before him, she had almost lost her mind from losing a man that tortured and physically abused her off and on for three and a half years. She had spent months withdrawing from the addiction that her past relationship had given her.

With him, she was ready to settle down. Though she was young she wanted to be married and happy. She had known the importance of love and felt the reality of pain. Both affected her life. She dreamed of love in every way but could never seem to grasp it. Her previous relationship had shaped her and molded her into something she wasn't even conscious of. Communication had been destroyed, her heart shattered, and she was now connected with the winter.

She was soft as cotton and could be as nonchalant as a man, some would say. Some could not fathom going through all she had experienced and still believe in love yet knowing when to retreat. She could lay with a man and feel no sentiment, though she preferred that they feel admiration for her. They often did. She was a mystery to them.

After months of twisting and turning, she had finally decided to let go of her old self. She didn't think she was quite ready for a relationship when she met him. He was a dream come true. He dreamed about love and wanted a family just as she did. For the first time, she was going out of her way to see him. To hear him. To smell his body. She smiled every time he was mentioned. She ran into him twice by coincidence and, in a couple of weeks, she had his keys. They were going to get married. He was the one, she had told her family. He was different. The way he could bring out the kid in her, the way he hugged her, the way she could be herself around him. He loved the love stories, too. He wasn't easily impressed, but he admired her. She was fascinated by him. He did not flock to her knees the way the others did.

She doesn't quite remember when or how it all fell apart. Maybe it was when he called the wedding off, or their first argument. It had been such a short time and she felt so connected to something that was going so wrong, so fast. This was not what she needed. She couldn't handle another loss of something that seemed so perfect. The arguments became deeper and more painful. There was a tongue war and each cut was silently destructive. But she was afraid to be alone so she stayed. She was determined to find it back. They had their moments. The songs he'd let her hear to show her how he felt, touched her. Most of the time, there were walls building. Walls she had no control over. Though they seemed to have so much chemistry, they clashed some- where in between. Something had gone wrong. Maybe she wanted it too bad, or maybe not bad enough. Maybe they were too much alike.

Sometimes she'd sit and look at him to try and read his mind. It was as though his thoughts were his most intimate moments that she had wanted to be a part of. She'd hang on the tips of his tongue, just in case he decided to say something meaningful. Like a daughter yearning for a father's attention, she yearned for his words, his expressions, his emotions. She listened for the beating of his heart, the unspoken brokenness, and declarations of love. They rarely appeared and she had grown empty. Silently frustrated. He seemed to be looking for more than she could give him. Her beginnings of prayer and dedication to God did not ignore the fact that she still wanted him.

The cab was $75 between the packing and the drive to her home. She tried to fight the tears but couldn't. This was all too familiar—this failure thing. It wouldn't have hurt so bad if she hadn't let go so soon. For God's sake, she had kissed him and meant it. Maybe she told him too much and he lost respect for her. Maybe she didn't tell him enough. This was it for her. She was going to wait until God dropped a man from the sky. She popped in her *The Best of Sade* CD and began to unpack again. It was hours before the phone rang and her heart began to beat too fast. She didn't have anything to say.

"Hello?"

"Girl, are you alright? I called home and you weren't there so I figured you were here." The annoying sound of her nosy girlfriend relieved her.

"Yeah, girl, you know I'm okay. I gotta be. It was just time to go, you know."

"Yeah, I know. You always putting yourself through some bullshit. You didn't get to know him, anyway. Leave it to you to love them and leave them alone!"

"I gotta go. I'm tired." She was tired of her girlfriend's criticism when she never seemed to be able to keep a man to even talk about.

"Okay, suit yourself. Call me so we can go niggah huntin' next week."

"Okay, bye." She hung up quickly, not even giving her friend a chance to say goodbye. She wanted to call him but she didn't. She lay down on a bed that she knew she would have to find comfortable again. Then came the knock on the door.

"Come in." She knew it was probably her friend from upstairs and she always kept her door open. She turned around and saw that it was him. He sat on her bed and looked at her. He was studying her the way she always studied him. It was unusual and scary. The way he had studied her when he first met her. There was the sparkle again. The one she'd waited on for months. She opened her mouth but nothing came out.

"You don't have to say anything anymore. I know what you're trying to say. I can find you wherever you are now.

"I know how to pull you out now. I can read your mind and we can die together so that we may love again. So that we may live again," he continued. "Nothing's worth a goodbye if it's so right. Right? All we need is a little faith. We believe, don't we? Are you ready?"

"No," she answered. And she left with him with whatever she had.

Slip

Slip Forever

Abyss
Permed Hair
Nails with dollar bills
Fantasy
Dolls dressed
Wedding bells
Sex
Stilettos
The White world

Panties

These yellow
With red spots
White
With red spots
Black
With red spots

Professors

Teach me to say yes
Yes sir, ma'am you always be right
While I lose my mind
To your philosophies of life

Seven days

Long nights
Silence
By the number seven
Seven days
I cried
And screamed
Until I realized

Why

Y is stupid to me
Too many words for Y

Toxic

You
Your passion
Your passionate love
Your passionate love stings
Your passionate love stings bees

Mother

How confusing
Mother can be
Nurturing
Destructive

Daddy

She called you daddy
Even when you weren't there

Man's Pleasure, Woman's Pain

She waited in the wings of the hotel lobby for him to come. He never did. She went home and turned the volume up on the phone but it never rang. The next morning would be too late. Sandra's daughter, Angel, would be coming home from vacation with her father and though Sandra missed her, she could no longer hide that she missed him more. Every day had become harder—harder for her to hide the way she felt. She thought that by having Angel she could take her mind off of him, but she never stopped thinking.

"Breathe," she would often say to herself.

She would look into Angel's eyes and wonder why hadn't someone so beautiful taken away the emptiness. Why she still could feel his presence Just as she began to go outside of her body, the doorbell rang.

"Mommy, it's me. I'm home."

She opened the door and Angel jumped on her, giving her a big kiss.

"Hello, baby, how was you and daddy's trip?" she asked.

"Oh, Mommy, I had so much fun! I saw Mickey Mouse and Minnie. She wasn't all that pretty and Mickey had these big ears. They were funny, Mommy."

Sandra, engrossed in the disappointed look of her husband, says, "Yeah, baby, sounds like fun. I know you must be sleepy from that plane ride so go and get changed into something comfy so you can tell Mommy all about it."

She watched as Angel sings the Disney song all

the way to her room. Then turned to her husband.

"What's the look for? Been gone a whole week and you're still not happy with me. Well, you said you needed some time to think, Kyle, so did you?"

"You didn't even call, Sandra. Not once. Not to find out if I was alive or even your daughter, for God's sake. Are you that gone that you don't even give a fuck about your family?"

Sandra laughed. "Oh, Kyle, grow up. I had a life before you. Do I need to talk to you every second in order for you to feel secure?"

"You never change, Sandra. I was just too in love to see. It's my fault. I knew you weren't in love with me. I was just hoping…"

"Hoping what?! That you could turn me into your little sex kitten or concubine who says 'Yes Sah' whenever you wanted? Well, guess what, Kyle. It all backfired. Just because you put these clothes on my back or because you can afford a diamond ring or two doesn't guarantee you me. You think you can buy me a Mercedes every year and that will get you another year with me. Well, you have to earn this."

"From day one, you were the same little selfish bitch you are now. Sandra, that's it! I'm through. I'm taking Angel and getting far away from you and your demented sick self."

Kyle called for Angel. "Angel, baby, daddy is going to take you on another trip."

"And where do you think you are taking my baby?" screamed Sandra.

Kyle aggressively walked up to Sandra as though he were going to hit her. She flinched. He stopped right in front of her face and said, "Do me a favor. Don't act like you care."

She fell into the seat behind her as she watched Angel's eyes going out the door with her father.

"That bastard!"

It wasn't until 10 p.m. when the phone rang.

"Hey, baby."

"Harold!...Don't 'hey baby me.' What happened to you?" she asked.

"Damn, baby, I'm sorry. I got caught up with the fellas. So I see you talkin'. Must mean the hubby didn't come back yet."

"Yeah, he done came and went. He had the nerve to take Angel with him. I don't know what he thinks he can do with a four-year-old little girl. He'll be back."

"I don't know, Sandra, you ain't been the best woman, especially fuckin' wit me. You know I be tearin' that shit up, girl."

Sandra giggled. "Whatever, niggah."

"Yo, I'm downstairs. Come down here so I can get a good look at that fine ass."

"Gimme a second." Sandra threw on some Estee Lauder perfume and her flats and ran downstairs. She looked for Harold's BMW. She hoped he hadn't just finished smoking weed. She hated the smell.

"Get in," he said, startling her. "You okay, baby."

Something about the way he said that brought tears to her eyes. "That's why I love you, because you always cared. It has been ten years and I can still talk to you. You make me feel special—like I'm not the average girl."

"That's because you're not. And I swear if Fleshia

wasn't so damn crazy, you would be my lady. But the kids need me at home."

"Yeah, I understand. I'll wait till the time is right. You are the only one who knows. You saved my life. If you hadn't come that night, I don't know what would have happened. I owe you me. I owe you everything." Sandra stared into his eyes with gratitude.

He touched her face. "You know, if I ever find out who that nigger is that did that to you and left you to die like that, I would kill him."

"I know. After that day, I never felt comfortable again. I can't even make love to Kyle. Only you. It's something about you."

She kissed him. Then tore open his shirt to kiss his chest. She looked up at him and then down again. She went deeper and deeper until she felt his pants. She unbuckled them and reached in for his pleasure. She stroked and kissed.

He oohed and ahhed and remembered the day she wore that pink mini-skirt. He remembered that tender 18-year old virgin flesh and how it felt through her screams. He remembered hitting her just enough to hurt her without saying a word. He looked at her plump watermelon breasts through that black stocking cap—the ones he noticed for days. He remembered saying that he wanted it again.

"Baby, let me hit it from the back."

Sandra lifts up and turns around in an awkward position in this small BMW. He finally penetrates. She feels different—almost like sobbing.

"OOOH, baby, that feels good," as he pumped.

She couldn't control her tears now.

"Damn, baby you got the best pussy in the world."
She hoped he can't see her.

"Back that up some more. I want to feel every-thing."

She willingly backed up though the seat belt is cutting through her legs.

"I'm about to come. Stay right there," he says as he gives a loud moan and plops on top of her.

The seatbelt pressed against her stomach so hard she couldn't speak. It's as though something ha her tongue. And he was going so fast that he hurt her. She wanted him to get off of her. She wanted to tell him that she didn't want to do this anymore. That she was tired of repaying him—that she knew he didn't love or respect her. She wanted to say that she never really enjoyed his body odor and his sex never did satisfy her. She wanted to scream but instead she thought, " I miss Angel and if I could only love Kyle."

Savior

He lifts my hand and cries like nights are riding high through the summer breeze. Riding to the moonlight sky is what he does when he cries. Cries Jesus done need to rescue me cause that harlotry has some spirituality. Ride with me to heavenly memory that rides through the Black skies till Jesus can stop his cries.

This Too Shall Pass

Baby Father's comin' home

Bap!!

I ain't got no money

Damn!!

Scared to go outside

Boom!!

Gonna mess up my car

Bam!!

He left me with his baby boy

Shh!!

Baby Boy

I TOLD HIM HE HAD TO GO
Downtown, Uptown…
Whatever suited his soul

'Cause it WASN'T me

He put his hands on me
And I promised that was going to be the last of history
He could Go and find another woman

'Cause it Wasn't gonna be me

He lied and proclaimed sincerity
That he was a gentleman
Who brought candy, flowers, and rings
BUT didn't mind having his WOMAN
Take care of him

I wish he would have told me this sooner
'Cause it Wasn't gonna be me

He was a MASTER in game
A MASTER in affection
A MASTER in talk
A MASTER in bed

But it Wasn't good enough for me

Kisses

It only tells a tale of who she was. If only she had kissed them, they would have known. It had haunted her not knowing the permanence of a man's touch. Her legs quivered at the awakening of their entrance. She had it all—so they said—something that separated her from the rest. It was not in her wealth but in her classiness that they could never piece the puzzle. She could make bubbly brown eyes deceive her and she thought she could break a man's heart with her body. Never consciously, of course. She had mastered the game…or the game had mastered her. It had taught her the importance of loving hard yet less, friendly yet cold, heartful still watchful, and sexy not sleazy.

When she dressed she took her time. She lotioned her 5'6" full-figured body, observed her skin, and often caught herself staring in the mirror. She rarely thought about them. Even when she knew they were not thinking about her. Victoria's Secret was for Mondays. Bath and Body Works were Tuesdays, and every other day always made up their own mind. Many nights she found herself not being able to dress alone. She always had someone watching her. Though she had claimed her own territory, she found herself escaping for seconds of peace to a place where her eyes could belong to themselves.

Her friends and family asked why she was so fickle. She posed a mystery to them. Not because she was damaged goods or because she had intended to cover any skeletons form her past. Nor was she a father-less child. She loved her father and her father loved her more than life itself. As far as her mind could go back, she never remembered needing. Her father represented 100 percent man—a hard competition for the others.

The men wondered why their moments were so temporary. No matter what they had to offer, it was never enough. The jewelry, the cars, the promises only made her ask for more space. She didn't care if they left. Even the sex did not carry too much weight. She felt that it had served its purpose—a convenient high. Sometimes she wanted it real bad and sometimes she'd wished she never wanted it at all. So there were moments she felt nymphotic and others were spent alone. In her seldom solitude, she would cook for herself, light a candle, take long bubble baths, and sleep in her lingerie. She did her best work when she was alone. She said that she'd rather it be this way so that she could not be accused of breaking any hearts.

Tony made her Mondays go by quicker and Ricky made her Wednesdays sexier. Whoever she spent her Fridays with frequently won the prize of her weekend. She shared her body with all of them and each of them offered her something unique. She studied them—recognizing their flaws and strengths. She always let them talk until they eventually talked out of their heart. She possessed the gift of being able to pull out delicate information without giving her own. She gave them just enough for them to want her. They wanted her exclusively, which she had so often brushed off. She carried pieces of them and cherished each piece without letting it get attached. It was just enough for her to get by.

She knew she had something more to offer than what they always saw first. But she could never let them find out. She could teach them how to really love, she said, not only in her sex but also in the ways her words wrapped around their egos, the way her mind stroked their pride, and the way her body caressed their emotions. She would never hurt them, she claimed, though they had not always vowed the same with her. And why should they have to? Who was willing to give their all to a mystery? Who was willing to settle for the detached? After a while, their frustration became anger. When she realized they had come to this point, she quickly tried to replace. But replacing was not always easy—especially when it involved a man's heart. Though she often succeeded, she wore the bruises and pondered on why she had to go. Some thought she enjoyed hunting and no longer feared the blood. Some say that it was her innate being that always played the game. She said that they just couldn't see because they had never gotten close enough. She, with her fire-red Ann Taylor suit and four-inch pumps, walked down Lexington Avenue to her daily job at the advertising agency. She was thinking on her current campaign for the new Donna Karan women's line when she spotted out of the corner of her eye a tall Latina woman wearing black stilettos and a mini skirt that revealed a sparkling silver thong. This woman is confident, she thought, as the Latina woman caught every man's eye. Then she thought about an idea for the campaign: "Sexy Yet Confident—The Ultimate Woman." Karen stared at the woman in admiration. One man in particular caught Karen's eye. He was looking intensely at her.

Karen walked over to him and said, "Something on my face?"

"I was just trying to figure out what you're made of."

"Well, it's going to take more than just a glance." She was in awe of his dimples and chocolate-brown complexion. His Armani suit hugged his medium-built figure. She wanted him for Friday, she thought.

"Dinner at Carmines, 8 p.m. Friday?" he asked

"Sounds like a plan. I'll meet you in front," she smiled.

Just as she began to walk away, she turned and said, "By the way, it's Karen and I have a rule that I don't give out my number until after the first date."

"Oh, how rude of me. Carl. I work right over here at Paine Webber and your rules are mine, too."

She slowly backed away, nodded her head in satisfaction, and headed toward Park Avenue. Her mind wandered to her busy schedule—meeting at 12, luncheon at 2, dinner at 6, and since today is Wednesday, she thought, she might just try Gary again. He always updated her with the daily news, good new books, movies, and songs. Plus, she liked his taste. He had a style of his own and his conversation stimulated her. Before meeting Carl, she figured she'd go to Macy's to get a new perfume.

Carl thought about how he was going to get out of the jam he was in. The economy was down and slowly but surely clients were pulling their money out of their accounts on a daily basis. He assured himself that he would be back to his usual $250,000 salary soon. Karen interested him. He saw something in her that he had not seen in a long time—strength, boldness, and independence. She was class with a capital C, he thought.

It had been almost three years since he was in a

serious relationship, and the closest he had come to one was the girls he was given by his company on those foreign trips. Unlike his colleagues, he always treated the girls with respect. He took them shopping, cooked for them, and gave them good conversation. Sometimes he didn't even touch them. He called them his "short-term friends." Because they were strangers, he found it easy to share secrets with them.

Carl never really got to know his mother. He heard only that she was a prostitute—a high-class one. Rumor was that basketball players, senators, and CEOs requested her. He remembered her only visiting him on holidays. She always came in with a bag full of gifts. He was "in love" with her and thought that there could never be anyone as pretty as his mother. He used to stare at the way she walked and her beautiful dresses. In the winter, she wore mink—a white one with black spots on it. No matter how disappointed he was in her, as soon as he would see her, all his disappointment subsided. He loved her soft voice and silky hands, and he clearly remembered that bright red lipstick. She was eloquent. He never wanted her to say goodbye but she always did and was gone too long. He saw her for the last time on his sixteenth birthday, before hearing that she had been murdered. Her last words were something he could never forget.

"Your mother's not a bad woman, Carl. Don't be mad at me for leaving like this all the time. Life has made me this way. Every day I see your face…every day. When all is said and done, people are gonna respect your momma. I'm gonna make sure you have everything you need so you'll have enough money to take care of that lucky woman you will marry. You'll be able to take care of her and me when I can't do it no more. Okay, baby."

She walked out the door and he ran to the window as he always did so he could watch her walk away. She looked up at the window and blew her normal goodbye kiss and said, "You're the only man I ever kiss."

He was ever grateful to his father who had raised him and taught him the value of respecting women— even when they do unrespectable things. His father would say, "It's something special about anything or any- one who can give birth and unless you can do it, I don't want to hear anything negative out of your mouth." Even when Carl realized he was with the wrong woman, he never tried to hurt her. His friends said that he shouldn't try to save a dirty woman's soul. But he tried—he tried to save them. He wanted to show them how beautiful life could be. And who better to see it than a woman—the giver of life.

Karen reminded him of his mother. It was in her eyes. He'd try to be discreet about it but it couldn't be removed from his mind. Prematurely, he was already planning where they would vacation this summer. Maybe in Jamaica or the Bahamas or Paris. He wanted to take her somewhere she had never been. But he knew that she was a woman of many worlds. Her walk revealed that her sexual experience was mature and he wanted to explore her. He wanted to take her in front of a huge mirror and tell her what was so beautiful about her. Most of all, he wanted to kiss her. He already knew, before any conversation, that her kisses were to be shared only with a few.

All that I could be…

I wanted to reach out and heal them
And that's why I fancied them

I wanted to remove the memory
Of the crackhead or abusive mother
Of the absent, distant, or reckless father
Of the abandonment in their life

And that's why I stuck around so long

I wanted to erase the loss
And replace with my presence

I wanted to capture
What they would never say to any other woman
But me

I wanted to be their niggah and lover too
And put down their blunts, drinks, and hands
And pick up the family and home I was going to pro-
vide

I wanted to heal a couple of them at a time
By telling them with my body
How much they were worth

I wanted them to change their hearts around
And love exclusively
To be invited to a place of contentment and inner peace
Fearing God
Somewhere they finally belonged
Something that was their own
Despite their inability

I wanted to push their dreams
Let them experience their fantasies
Even if it was at my expense

I wanted their children to see how beautiful their future
step-mother could be
In absence of their fathers

I wanted to build
Even if I was the only one with the materials

I didn't want to start all over again
"So I would heal them"
I would say
"Heal them with my pain"

I want to be all that I can be
To everyone
But me

Petite

I know you like petite women
But my full-figured body can do acrobatics, too

Maybe my breast can oversatisfy you
But my mind can, too
I promise to never underestimate the man in you

Maybe you like those flat abs and small thighs
And I'm a lot to hold on to
But I can feel petite upon your entrance

I just want you to enjoy the ALL in me
I just want you to like the inside of me

I know ideally I might not be your type
Size two
But when you get to know me
I'll be seven times better than that two

Besides, I can teach you a thing or two
About the tricks big women can do

I just want you to enjoy the ALL in me
I just want you to like the inside of me

I know it gets real warm when you hug me too long
And real full when you squeeze

Black Dresses Stain

It'll be real good when you're engrossed in me
Real truth when we kiss
(And since I can deal with the fact that your lips are
bigger than mine without being scared, you can deal
with me, too)
'Cause I'll have you real open when you realize what
you have in me

I just want you to enjoy the ALL in me
I just want you to like the inside of me

And while you are enjoying the petiteness of my inner
body
Don't forget to fall in love with the full-figured me

In Transition

Sometimes I think about us and our short-term connection. Though I was married with a child and he content in a newfound love, he remained an integral part of my life like all the Lees that had come and gone. It was those silent nights, midnight bathroom breaks, and quiet kisses on my daughter's face as she peacefully slept when I would remember him.

He and I seemed to share each other's emotions. We were the product of each other's pain. When I wanted to see myself, I would look at him, stare, and study him. It was a wonder why our three-month relationship was filled with extreme ups and downs. For a while, we created our own little world where we hated everyone else (because they were so unrealistic and phony). Then, we began to look at ourselves—our lives, miserable, unfulfilling relationships, and our short-lived victories. Both of us fell out of grace with our mothers, fell in love with the wrong people, and fantasized for a moment over what could be but never was. And we depended on and searched for what never existed in either of us.

I, broken and recovering from cancer, had become incapable of expressing emotion and having effective communication. I was just learning that I was a lady again. I was remembering how to take care of myself and my hygiene. I, retired from femininity, appreciated life for the hour and not the day. Unfortunately, I had been in competition with all the other ladies in his life. Though we were learning about and growing in God together, in the end, it seemed as though He had let us both down.

We learned, through each other, how deeply life had hurt us. When he sopped talking, I wanted to tell him how much I loved and needed him. But when I tried, nothing ever came out. When I did decide to speak, I defended myself and criticized him.

And we tried, almost cried, screamed, and fought before we would catch ourselves. I professed that crying was for the weak and kissing for the dumb—as we built each other's walls.

I never wanted to leave him. We had too much to offer each other—but neither ever did. I packed my clothes but inside, I wanted to make us work. I wanted to beg him to stay and grow old with him. But my pride was too stubborn.

As soon as I moved out, he moved on. I went out of my way to see him—but he acted as if I wasn't there.

I can't tell you how he stopped loving me and how I continued to love him. I can only say that it was the start of my hair falling out in the middle of my head. It was the last time I colored my hair or wore bright red lipstick. It was the beginning of me taking on men as projects—assignments in transition.

Worthy "Projects"

She got up at 9 a.m. and was dressed by 10. She figured that since everyone was only interested in her cap and gown, who cared about what she wore underneath. She threw on some black jeans, a white t-shirt of her estranged husband, and some boots with heels. She hated wearing makeup but wouldn't dare leave the house without some lip gloss on since her mother would have a fit if her face was too bare. She didn't have to get there till twelve. She thought about how she had made it this far. In a couple of hours, she would officially be Dr. Evelyn Saunders. Too bad she didn't feel like a doctor. "Doc- tors are supposed to have the ability to heal people. And I'm stuck," she thought. She thought about her husband, who had just left the night before, and wondered whether he would show up at her graduation. She sat around and stared at the blank television until it was time for her to leave.

She insisted on driving herself to the ceremony so that she would not be nervous and it would give her the opportunity to think, but all she could think about was Sean. She never really discovered whether she ever loved him or if he was there to fill the void or if the idea of marriage had taken over her mind and started to sound good. She knew he had a woman—everyone knew. They had been separated for over a year and Sean had a woman (or two) about a week into the separation. They had a volatile relationship. If they weren't arguing, they were fighting and if they weren't fighting, they were fucking—and it never went beyond this. Finally, he stopped coming home and before she knew it, he was living somewhere else.

It wasn't always like that. Before she got pregnant with their daughter, he waited on her hand and knee. He cooked, cleaned, brought her flowers, paid the rent, and was all man in the bedroom—concerned only with pleasing her. It took him only about six months to start his disappearing acts, but by then she was already pregnant. He couldn't tell her what the first three months of his daughter's birth life was like because he wasn't around. But he could say that as soon as he came back around she let him in with open arms. Unfortunately, she realized that forgiveness could not be granted in a touch nor could a man's tears determine his ways.

Sean would pick up his daughter at least once or twice a week and call and talk to Susan whenever he needed an ear. Evelyn always listened even when he was disrespecting her or if the conversation involved taking off her clothes. Often, he'd pursue her for casual sex. She could never understand how something that she thought was so strong and committed had become so casual. At first, she would be hurt after he'd sleep with her and then flaunt his girlfriend in her face. Later, she just accepted it for great sex-on-call.

"The sex is good," she would say. "If he really loved them, why would he continue to sleep with me? Besides, I am his wife," she would explain when asked.

She wanted to divorce him but felt that maybe one day things would turn around and be the way they used to be. Coming from a home in which both parents had divorced and remarried, she knew she did not want this for her daughter. No matter how many times Sean had stolen from her, used her, cursed her out—she was hopelessly opening her door for him again and again. Part of her enjoyed being by herself (as long as it wasn't too long) and the other part couldn't deny the pain of his absence. His absence had become too familiar to her. Whenever she needed him, he was nowhere to be found—summer months, her birthday, and so on. She was so embarrassed when her neighbors could hear them fight or he'd storm out the door or when one of her friends told her they had seen him with another woman. But she always came up with the perfect excuse: "He's just really stressed out now" or "He had a bad day at work" or "That was just his friend from school." It was never his fault and in some way she was responsible—at least she would tell herself so.

She was in no way perfect, she would admit. She had needs, too, and every now and then, when she got tired of waiting on Sean or his broken promises, she would go back to an old flame or try to embrace a new one. She said that it was her way of protecting herself by all means necessary. Sean once said, " You with a PhD can't even keep me. Now ain't you pitiful." She cried over those words too many times. She had accepted a man who had barely earned his GED and he found joy in disgracing her.

"Pain…the Mrs. never experiences pain cause she got it all together with her Lexus Jeep, high-paying job, and PhD. The Mrs. deserves to be treated like a queen. Maybe some old weak college boy will do," he'd laugh.

"No," she sighed, "I just want you…I want us the way we used to be."

And he'd laugh as if she was telling a hilarious

joke to a receptive crowd.

"Your problem is, baby, that you don't smile enough. You know you look much better when you smile. You can be so pretty if you just smile a little bit. Things are so much easier when you close your mouth and chill out," he said.

These words were just enough to buy him a night at her place where he was almost guaranteed to leave early the next morning after swearing her to silence about the night before and asking her to borrow a dollar or two. She knew the night was temporary but she said that she wanted to feel good—even only for a night. She said that this was the only time she could make him sweat and that was enough satisfaction for her.

She threatened to divorce him but she knew that it was too hard for her to do and he was too broke to pay for one. It was her way of saving her hopes in their marriage. Maybe one day he would love her again.

She arrived at the school just in time for her march down the aisle on to the podium. This doctorate of psychology class of 2004 was comprised of all women and though she protested the male speaker, she was unsuccessful. As soon as she took her seat, she started searching for Sean.

"I can't believe him...one of the most important days of my life and he's late," she muttered.

Noticing the look on Evelyn's face, Dr. Banks, her long-time advisor and mentor, asked, "What's wrong? Is everything okay?"

"I'm alright. Have you seen my family?"

"Yeah, your mother and daughter are over there."

"Oh, yeah, thanks," she answered, trying not to

uncover the fact that she was not looking for them.

She knew Sean was going to pull this. Whenever she had loaned him her Jeep, he always showed up late, if at all.

"He promised he would be here," she whispered to herself.

But Dr. Banks heard her and he knew she wasn't looking for her family. He had tried to tell her for so long that Sean was no good for her (in so many words). All the late-night conversations about her ability and talent never convinced her. Sometimes he felt like slapping her in the face and saying, "Wake up. Don't you see what he is doing to you?" But he knew that harsh words never won an ear. So he sadly watched a young woman he valued as a daughter, throw her heart away. Even her other professors saw her potential. They proclaimed that she never needed a PhD—that reading people was her gift. Dr. Banks knew that it was a curse that she could see and solve everyone else's problems except for her own.

The service had gone by quickly. Mr. Brown had risen to speak:

"Today we are here to witness the power of a woman's words. A woman needs no PhD to acknowledge that with the power of her tongue, she can build a boy into a man…"

As far back as she could remember, Evelyn was expecting and pushing for the best out of Sean. She registered him for college, bought him his first diamond jewelry, and bailed him out of financial troubles more than once. Whenever he'd lose a job, she'd hunt till she found him one. He would wait until unemployment almost run out and say, "It's the White man's fault when they started paying Black women more money and giving them all the jobs. Now a brotha like me don't have no opportunities." Even though he was not helping her sup- port their daughter, she would pity his plight and offer her assistance.

And he was not the first. She paid for Ricky's induction into the fraternity, bought Alan his first suit and pair of shoes, took Donald to his first restaurant and even took him out the country for the first time in his life. She always wanted to give them the best—expose them to the other side of life. She wouldn't even know what to do if someone started to treat her better than she treated them. When she did find someone who tried, something was wrong. Such as he wasn't fine enough or tall enough or good enough in bed. One cop bought her peach-colored roses once a week, and he was weak. The professor she dated who spent valuable time trying to know her mind (apparently for too long) was gay. The lawyer who took her on romantic outings and bought her her first diamond was too conceited and would leave her for a white woman later. There was always an excuse. Instead she chose to stay with what Dr. Banks called, "projects." She hoped that she could change the 'F' into a 'C' and then finally the 'C' into an 'A'—even if the "project" took years. She took on all kinds of projects—players, abusers, alcoholics—just to say she had the ability to make a man.

"But before we go out and heal the world, my sisters," Mr. Brown spoke in between Evelyn's thoughts, "We must love and heal ourselves. We must know our worth."

And on those words the crowd stood up in

applause—everyone except for Evelyn. Sean had just arrived and she could see his face in the last row. He winked at her. She stared at him.

"A woman's worth," she thought.

She stood up to join the crowd in the standing ovation. Sean was talking on the cell phone when they called her name for her degree. Dr. Banks shook her hand firmly with tears in his eyes and said, "You don't know how special you are, Evelyn, but one day you will." Though not a part of the program, she grabbed his arm to give him a hug and cried on his shoulder.

"Thank you, for everything," she responded, overwhelmed by emotion.

She felt pride in herself that she had made it thus far, practically alone. She was thankful of the support of her parents and wanted to show her daughter that nothing was impossible. When the ceremony was over, she headed over to kiss her mother and daughter and then went up to Sean.

"Congratulations, baby," he said. "Now you are really the shit with a PhD. The more I look at you the more I realize how much I need you."

"When did you realize you needed me, Sean? When you showed up almost two hours late for my graduation? Or when you drove around in my Jeep last night and brought it back to me without any gas? Or when you forgot to pick up our daughter from my mother's this morning?"

"Come on, baby," Sean groaned. "Today is your day. I just want you to be happy. Can you please not bitch with me today? Everyday you just bitch, bitch, bitch. When you gonna learn to shut up and go with the flow?"

"Today," she calmly answered and began walking over to her mother and daughter to go to the Jeep.

Sean followed her. "Yo, what the fuck is wrong with you?"

"Nothing, Sean. I just don't see my worth in your eyes—I never saw it."

"Yo, call me when you get over this bullshit." Sean stormed out of the building.

Evelyn stayed in the same spot for about five minutes as if his leaving had paralyzed her. Usually she'd follow him out the door and beg him to stay or tell him to come over later on tonight so they could talk. She ran over to her daughter and mother, kissed them on the cheek, and walked them out the door to her new silver Lexus Jeep. She jumped in the car, breathed deep, looked at her daughter in the back seat, and said, "This is what Mommy's worth and someday you will know, too."

She caught Dr. Banks from the corner of her eye and he came over for a final hug.

"Don't be a stranger, kiddo. My home and office will always be yours," he said. "Plus I have some projects I might need your help with."

"No, Dr. Banks," she said. "I'm not looking for anymore projects…only full-time opportunities."

He smiled with satisfaction and approval and said, "It's about time."

Infinity

I shouldn't let him come up in me like that
Take advantage of my space
To manipulate my purpose

I shouldn't let him slip him in my heart like that
Accepting that he was less
Trying to make him more
More of the man that he didn't want to be

Now my breasts are feelin' sore
And stomach is a swollen brown
But he ain't nowhere around

This is number four for me
This odyssey of not knowin' my worth

He say he can only take my mouth when I'm kissin him
My mind when I'm agreein
That I am too opinionated
Complex

My breasts got too big for him
My sex not freaky enough
'Cause I want to be made love to
But he wanted it rough

I didn't make him feel like a man
When I talked, walked, stared, whatever

Black Dresses Stain

I shouldn't let him underappreciate my exposure
My queenly, diversified culture
My head was too high
Yet esteem hung down low

And I was blind
To the pattern

For this was number ten for me
This iniquity of not knowin' my worth

Too often I had believed his lies
And burdened myself
With his broken past and unsure future
I shared me
Like we were already "one"

I had too many clothes
Too many shoes
Too much of everything that reminded him of the more
woman in me
And the less man in him

For I with a bachelor's degree
Had mapped out my destiny
While he with a GED
Made excuses for why he wasn't where he was sup-
posed to be

He talked of the "habit" that ran throughout the family
Or the father he missed
Or the numerous states he stayed

He talked of bad relationships
Growing up under the streets

I shouldn't have let him talk to me
About all his backed-up shit
Yet he said he didn't know how to communicate with
me
So he'd rather go back to the beginning of his history

A history marked with pain and shame
Everything that I was trying to get him not to be

I shouldn't let him slip in my heart like that
Accepting that he was less
Trying to make him more
More of the man that he didn't want to be

Now my breasts are feelin' sore
And stomach is a swollen brown
But he ain't nowhere around

This is number infinity for me
Me not knowin' my worth

Celibate With A Seed

For so long, I, professional, church-going woman, promised God I would give it up for him. But my flesh told my mind that I had to fulfill my physical need. It made me feel whole-to be touched confidentially. So when I couldn't keep my promise, I promised to be selective with my choices. Even though these choices usually turned out to be the wrong ones, I kept trying and holding on as long as I could to avoid the interruption.

I ran back into him on the A train to Manhattan and though it wasn't instant, our distance interested me. He was like me—introspective, plotting, and hard to capture the heart and soul. The days we did spend together (before intimacy) were nice and calm- —a walk on the promenade, a talk at Junior's—and it took me only a couples of moments to recognize a king in him. A king undiscovered—a distinction—one I had not seen in many since Sam Lee. I occasionally picked him up in East New York. He had not become a product of his environment. His diction was proper and style neatly refined. And since we graduated from the same private Catholic high school, I assumed we had similar morals. I predicted him to be a carefully planned man even when those plans failed. While I was thinking about us and our perfect fairytale ending at our 2010 high school reunion, his mind wandered on something or someone he never discussed.

I, at this moment, was halfway to my healing— consciously searching, moral, spiritually sound, almost whole again, and wanting to fall so in love I would forget the year or day or pastime. I soaked up moments that were to be—moments we would share. I just needed the intimacy and, because he seemed to enjoy mine, we seemed perfect together. He didn't require too much time and I was in between dreams, so he didn't drain or waste mine. I was exclusive to him and he professed monogamy to me. When we were both ready, we agreed to take us further. I anticipated that moment.

Ordinarily the smell disgusted me but he smelled sweet even when he was slightly high. We were raw intimates and he aimed to please. I pondered on the future tricks I could pull out of my bag for him—tricks I missed because they had been packed away for so long. Our rare conversation was personal and his touch was sensual. He was a smooth dark chocolate and I called him my "tar baby." I respected him and let him kiss me…

In our moments of heat, we would see each other once or twice a week. Then the kisses became fewer and he stopped trying to please me. I found myself letting him in at midnight and letting him out in the morning. He wasn't married but I knew number two was a hard price to pay and not knowing where you stood at all was worse. The nights he never came or called, I realized that when he talked, it was only about him. I supported him and his future even when he wasn't sure about it. So when he finally confessed his other long-term relation with the "Great White Hope," I figured out that my tar baby had dismissed this African Queen. He was investing his time with her while I was building and focusing my energy on him.

I was so sure he would at least be supportive and loving. I was confidant he would see "family" when he looked at me. That he would break the tradition of infidelity and abandonment that he was so familiar with. I just knew that he would change his mind and realize what he was missing in me. That he would look deep inside himself and want to be all the man he could be for me, and for him. I had no doubt that we'd be spending a lot of time together because he was going to be so concerned about this outcome. I pictured him looking at me like he adored me—giving me kisses on my forehead and watching me sleep.

Instead he broke me—first with his words and then with his silence. Slowly, he set me back a couple of years to when healing had not yet begun. The message was clear. And when I couldn't comprehend, he never explained. I couldn't track his miles per hour but he ran so fast when I told him that I had given him something that was just between us—something that he could not give himself. His seed had consumed me.

I became the "Mad Black Woman." In his distinction, he could not see beyond visibility. He was not concerned with the goodness of my heart or the longing in my soul or the oral intimacy I shared with him. He did not value our bare sex. And though I had not yet stood before him naked, I hoped and wished on something that wasn't real—something that had not even existed. I did not know who this man was. I had not learned the truth about him. I found myself alone.

I learned how to scream again. Tweet's "You" stayed on heavy rotation. He even made me pull out Lauryn Hill, Sade, and Alanis Morrisette. And at three months, I sat in a Jill Scott concert and cried in a dark corner seat. At five months, I found out that it was going to be a baby boy. While I celebrated the soon-to-be existence of a soon-to-be Black man, I mourned the absence of another. These months were too quiet, too still. No phone calls or voluntary prayers. It seemed that when- ever I felt myself getting stronger, I would run into enthusiastic partners rubbing the belly of what was to become part of them. I wept at the thought of single motherhood—that he had overlooked my beauty— stepped on my crown—and disrespected my dignity.

I finally had fulfilled my promise with God. Bruised bad enough to be numb, I didn't want to be touched or caressed or seduced. I didn't want to think about love and its moments. I lost all that longing and needing and wanting that a new birth tends to bring. I forgot and wanted to forget how his touch felt. How his voice sounded when he confessed to be different. I flushed all the dreams and prepared myself for the process of healing.

He showed up maybe a day too late. Though I pre- tended as though it never hurt, I never looked him in the eyes too long. I laughed and befriended him as if he still wasn't hiding. I wanted him to sit down and let me talk about it. I wanted him to say he would make it right. That this time we would take things slowly. That he had matured overnight and finally recognized my worth. That "us" was important now. But he never mentioned it. I wanted to ask him "why?" but I knew the answer was more complicated. I understood that hurt people only know how to hurt people. I knew that something inside of him was broken. I wanted to know how raw intimates can so easily be pretenders. How could he take some- thing that I carried and treat it so carelessly? How could a new life also bring about a death inside of me?

Time passed and my seed grew. I loved the seed of him but also yearned for the wind to hit my thighs or a surprise kiss on my neck. I kept backing out of the dates and lost the numbers of prospects. When opportunity chased, I ran faster. Throughout my adulthood, I had periods of slipping in and out of celibacy but the passion of being felt by another always remained. He and his memories had stripped me of my desires. My only desire was to be whole again.

Missed Beginnings

We missed those beautiful beginnings that every couple needs-courtship, friendly games, the chase, butterflies in your stomach, etc. We started in the middle- after our child. The middle was awkward and we tried to catch up quickly but I'm sure we'd skip a thing or two. We lived like a family and I woke up to him almost every morning. He was a great father to our son and I adored the way he loved him.

But I wanted him to look at me that way he looked at our son. And even though our sex felt overwhelmingly pleasant and his presence fulfilled me, I wondered how this time was different. I wondered why he chose me so late. I did not say "I love you" when I first felt it for fear he would never feel the same way. But I had loved him even when he was with her.

Because we had missed beginnings, I could not trust his middle. I did not know his friends or what he did with his spare time on the weekends. I had not been invited to those special events that could possibly brought us closer or taught me too much. I had not learned his favorite color or other simple things that conversations were built around. I sensed unspoken pain, slight disappointments, and incomplete endings. I was not sure if it was because he missed her or if his experiences had made him this way.

I was still suffering from the way he broke me. So I had not fallen in love. I did not tell him too much or touch him too long. Because we had missed beginnings, I had silent insecurities. I questioned the validity of our intimacy. I questioned his affections and permanence.

He never gave me total assurance of anything except the moments. I was not sure if he had fully accepted my ready-made family or if our arrangement was one of convenience. I hoped that he'd grow to love the child that came of only me. He didn't say much about our new situation (at least nothing I wanted to hear). I wanted him to say that he never really loved her anyway- that I was always on his mind. But I knew neither was true. I saw the pictures of her and him vacationing in Cancun. He was taking pictures of her sleeping and brushing her teeth—so I knew there was love. When I was sick carrying his son, he was denying us.

There was a wall between us. Things we refused to say. Maybe my mind told me lies, but it seemed as if his smile wasn't as wide and laughter as deep. I cooked for him, gave him his space, enjoyed his TV programs, supported all his endeavors, listened to his dreams, and comforted his past. And no matter how many times he said "Thank you," I never felt like he meant it. He could not spend quality, quiet time with me. I made the most of borrowed time. But sometimes he was so quiet, I felt alone—so distant, I felt foreign.

Because we had missed beginnings, I never felt first. I knew if I hadn't had his son, I could have been easily dismissed. I felt like he had interrupted my peace and I had interrupted his love and freedom. I noticed that he was never fully attentive on important holidays—that he never followed up on his promises made around "us"— that he never carried his son's picture. But, at least, I thought his guilt has forced his loyalty to me.

While I was waiting for him to come home, inhaling

the Escada on his sheets, he was inhaling her. When he was in her presence, he called her his "girl." He acted as if he never said the word "family" to me. He let her call me a stupid bitch. He never acknowledged the birth of and love for our son. I never expected that he could not be the man he promised me—as if everything we had and the little we shared were based on lies.

I never wanted to take him back when he came around but I thought maybe he'd finally give me my missed beginnings. But even when he tried, I could not notice it. Because I did not look at him the same. And although I let him touch me, I could not forget how he made her feel just as good as he was making me feel. It disgusted me that even with a son I was no competition for her. That he shared with her what I was still working for—his time and intimacy.

Part of me felt empty, went limp, and wanted to be cold again. But I wanted us so bad I could taste it. I came close to baring my soul. I almost held him too long—loved him too much.

I wanted to run. I wanted to have a night of unadulterated sex with someone that was not so close to this confusion. I wanted to leave my kids behind for at least a week and go away with someone superfine and laugh hard again. I wanted to get my groove back with a man with a sexy foreign accent. Even if the feeling was temporary, I wanted to get him back and take pictures of it so he'd never forget. But subconsciously and regretfully, I had passed that stage of careless revenge and meaningless pleasures.

In forgiving him, I wanted to heal him. I wanted to tell him that everything was inside of me but I needed to see everything in him. But I don't even think he cared. I wasn't even sure if it was within him to love me the way I wanted to be loved. Because of his own personal bruises, I couldn't tell if any woman even mattered to him that much. When he vaguely shared emotions, I wanted to hang on the tip of his tongue to wait for more. But it never came. Maybe I expected too much from him. Maybe he was incapable of 100 percent heart and soul. So I engaged in conversation and accepted reply with our sex.

Since then, every moment together became a sacrifice. Every kiss involved a previous thought. Every word was a struggle. And I wanted to forget. I wanted to go back before our child and experience lust and love in its beginnings. I wanted an initiation process before things became so difficult—so real.

Fit To Be Queens

Shirley had four kids by four different men but didn't look a day older than forty with a Coca-Cola glass figure. This day was special since it was the first time she was going to see him in a year. She got all dressed up, put on her makeup, took an hour shower, and waited for him to come through the door. She knew he was coming because he put her address down as his place of residence prior to his release.

They had been through it all. Fifteen years of breaking up and making up—they were almost common law. She has stuck with him when he was buying fancy cars and clothes until he had officially become a petty street hustler. They shared her youngest child together and everyone knew the youngest was her favorite. Throughout the years, they moved in and out of state trying to make a better life for themselves. And they almost came close. But when they were consistently around each other too long, he would never treat her right.

So far, he had conceived two other children—one with her friend and another with a long-term mistress. Though it broke her heart that he continued to fool around outside of the good lovin she was giving him, she said that as long as he kept her first and never claimed the others she could forgive him. So he acted as if he had no more children and she acted as if he never cheated. She even caught a felony for beating up one of his other woman. And lost her right to vote. She said that history was deeper than anything and she wasn't going to let anyone take that history away.

Unfortunately, he never let her go too long. Just when she thought she might be ready to start over, he'd come back with a new, almost believable promise. But his promises always went unfulfilled and he'd blame it on her. "She gained too much weight" "didn't appreciate him" "stopped cooking" "too much mouth" or whatever excused his behavior for the moment.

So they ended up where they began—struggling, living paycheck to paycheck, her begging for his time and money—while she maintained a home on a part-time job and welfare check.

Brenda told her that she had enough skills to open her own beauty salon. She almost believed she could. She almost saved enough money but he came back at the right time with more "needs." She told herself that she was investing in his big payday. Now she was forty-five and the only thing that gave her satisfaction was her memories on when things were good and her reflection on the 1980's. Not even the look in her children's eyes could fix what she had missed.

"Besides," she said, "they all look different."

Brenda couldn't say too much. After twenty-five years of marriage, she found herself alone in a studio apartment. Her children were grown and she had to find other ways to occupy her mind. Her soon-to-be ex-husband had moved in with another woman in the house Brenda and he bought in their fifth year of marriage. She couldn't forget the day he told the police officer to move her out. And it wasn't for New York's marriage laws, she would have been homeless in a foreign land.

She left her hometown to make their relationship work. He, retired with a pension, watched her struggle on temporary assignments. But she tried to compensate in her cooking his breakfast promptly at 7 a.m., preparing the lunch he'd often throw away, maintaining an immaculate home, and having dinner on the table at 8 p.m. even when he didn't come home.

She went to church every Sunday morning while he watched sports and mocked "the crazy god she served." But even though she loved God, she knew that by the time she'd get home he would be drunk and he'd call her every name in the book except a child of God. Instead of getting revenge, she prayed for him. She prayed for herself—that God would cleanse her and forgive him just so she could subject herself to more of his abuse. She knew she had often let him go too far. That she should have left him a long time ago but old family values always told her to stay.

"You stay with that man no matter what. Marriage and love ain't easy. You have to work at it. He didn't mean it. You don't want your children growing up by themselves," she heard her mother say.

She thought God would punish her for forsaking her wedding vows. Plus, she wanted to give him time to change. But her never did. Matter-of-fact, things only got worse because when he stopped beating her, he started to verbally abuse her. And she made excuses for him. "His family life was messed up" "she wasn't supportive enough" "stress from the office" etc.

Her children watched her almost forsake them to please him. When they were young, they hated the fact that she was so passive. Every now and then, they'd disrespect her too—just because they knew they could get away with it.

Now she looked around and realized that though she was physically present, she had missed major events in their lives. And even though she provided their basic needs, they were emotionally motherless. Now she was sixty and they would barely visit her or return her calls. And she reminisced on the life she never lived.

When her youngest daughter, June, got her first apartment at 17, she begged Brenda to leave her father. But she couldn't gather the strength. Now she was depending on her mind, morals, the few friends he couldn't chase away, and God to keep her alive. And so far, she was surviving.

June, on the other hand, never cared about survival—only the moment. And maybe that's why she couldn't make up her mind whether she wanted to be with men or women. She was thirty and spent ten tender years with a man she was supposed to marry and watched him leave her for another woman. He was the first man she'd experienced and she wanted him to be the last.

But men had a place in her heart and she wanted biological children. Men offered her the challenge she needed. And she was always interested in why God had created such complex, seemingly unemotionally unattached creatures. She loved the games she could play with them because their needs were simple—sex, sports, food, ego, and pride. They gave her the protection she needed—the feeling of security and sensuality. And she loved it when they were tough and rough and almost unbreakable.

Women, on the hand, were just beautiful, soft, warm, innately all-caring and bearing. And she wanted to partake of their strength in more ways than one. She loved to see them cry and struggle then pull themselves together again.

"They were true listeners, natural sympathizers, and the reflection of different people in one body. They could turn on and off, if needed. They invented sacrifice and compromise," she would say.

She did not have to tell them her needs, wants, and desires. And she loved those mild-mannered, feminine, kind, compassionate types.

It was almost too simple the way men and women both loved and enjoyed her. The men thought her bisexuality was attractive. But she often lied to the women about her interest in both because they weren't always accepting.

She wanted to make a decision about what was really real. But she was in the prime of her life—having the time of her life. She didn't want to hurt anyone though she often did. And she got a little satisfaction in knowing that she had a choice. A choice she wasn't ready to make. Everything about her life now was spontaneous, spur of the moment, short term—and she wanted it like that.

She had missed her opportunity to become a mother when she lost her first love's child and though she had desire, she wasn't even sure if becoming a mother was in the cards. But she found herself seven months pregnant, by a local drug dealer who she didn't even know his last name. And he made it her business to forget her first. In the beginning, she tried to make it work with her long time fling, Tracey, who gave her needed comfort until the fifth month when she found out it was going to be a boy.

And because Lance was the only success, passive, and naïve man to be in her deck of cards around the date of her conception, she figured it was better to claim the baby was his. So Lance was happy that he had captured what he thought was unattainable and she pretended that this was the family she always wanted.

What was suppose to be considered a joy was unveiling so much pain. She only told her aunt Deborah the truth. She asked God to forgive her as she silently yearned for her careless, reckless lifestyle. She only told her aunt Deborah the truth. She asked he aunt to pray for her because she knew that since she was a pastor, her prayers availth much.

And even though her aunt Deborah was a pastor, it seems like God was answering everyone's prayers but Deborah's.

A surprise birthday was the furthest thing from Deborah's mind. She had hoped for a cruise or even a quiet evening for two. All night, she looked at the faces and painted her porcelain smile with an occasional rhythmic laugh. Jamal was always doing things like this. Last year, it was the Grand Ball dedicated in her honor. The year before it was 12 dozen roses with a celebration extravaganza for the whole neighborhood that lasted for a week. He showered her with diamonds, fur coats, anything that kept him from spending time.

Her voice never died... but faded with each passing year. Jamal became more but less important. She began to occasionally forget her freedom before him...before them. Every time she turned around, some-one was there—asking, wanting, needing. She wanted to tell them that she wanted and needed too. Her silence, once golden, had now become a moment of rest. Her thinking use to be so easy and unattached. Now it was connected to his...and the others.

I sat and watched. I knew that her wide-brim hats had hid her tears. I knew that she felt abandoned sometimes. I had seen the moments of mental escape. Those days when she smiled at me with a message. When I thought I was not able to recognize her anymore, I'd hold on to that message. I wanted to write her—but never could finish. When I started to pour out my heart, I felt so guilty that I had not lived up to the quota she set for me...and that I would become a member of them. How could I say that everything wasn't right?! That sometimes I'd felt that God had let us both down—in different ways.

That she had become Princess Diana to them...when she was Queen to me. And though, few gave her the proper crown, her name, Deborah, bore honor. She always looked like she stepped out of Vogue and wise words left her mouth. Even when her full-figure, dark skin was not initially well received, she could prove the crowds wrong because insightful oration came from her lips and left the people in awe. She demanded power when she walked whether it was elegant pumps or neat flats. Unfamiliar children picked up her kind com- passionate spirit and bruised and broken women could get partially healed in her hug. And I wanted her to get to the women. I wanted her to share her pain and triumphs with them to encourage them. I wanted to carry her on my shoulders and draw from her wisdom while sharing her with the streets. I wanted to scream and tell them that just because someone had snatched their crown didn't mean they weren't fit to be queens.

How good it feels
When your freedom comes back

Maybe I hadn't heard it
Until Jill Scott sang it
And my pastor taught it

Bills Overdue
No man
My path is cloudy
And credit bad

But I can feel breath in my soul again

I can hear my voice and see my tears
I can feel my smooth thighs rub one another
Like they are clapping
I can look in the mirror for extended periods
I can appreciate the air, trees, and birds again

Color has been restored to my soul

I don't care if the phone doesn't ring
Or if no one knocks on my door
Because I can appreciate my thoughts now.

Black Dresses Stain

Black dresses stain
no one can see them

She was touched in the wrong places
at the wrong times
by the wrong people
and black hands covered the scars

My people, even thugs, murderers
young and old
in the hood, courthouse
penthouse, church
are crying out
but few answer the call

She got shot in the heart
through her private parts
that should have been a life-giver
but brought her to a slow death

She stands
holds on
laughs
wears black dresses
so no one can see the blood

Chalet Jean-Baptiste

She starts all over
to another beginning
though she is at the end of her lifetime
goes through the motions
to an unfair
unequal world
and the black dresses make her look graceful
refined

Because black dresses stain
no one can see them
although it looks clean
you can smell the odor
feel its sting
black had been taught
to hide
run
move on

I am convinced
that all colors
probably stain
just as much
you can't see the pain
in the black ones

Made in the USA
Columbia, SC
16 June 2020